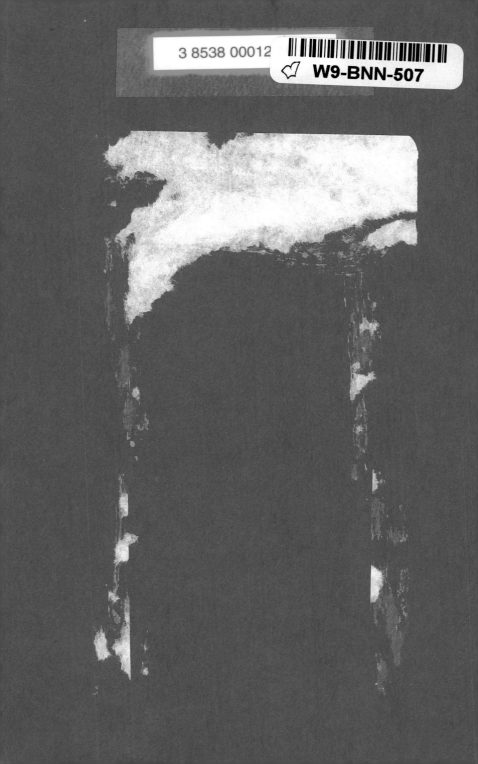

MAKING A
DIFFERENCE

MAKING A DIFFERENCE

The Story of an American Family

MARGARET HODGES

CHARLES SCRIBNER'S SONS • NEW YORK

ACKNOWLEDGMENTS

The author has based *Making a Difference* on Mary Beattie Sherwood's privately published *Living Recollections*, on letters and journals generously made available by the children of Jean Sherwood Harper, on personal interviews, and on correspondence with a wide circle of friends and admirers of a remarkable American family. She gratefully acknowledges the permission of Vassar College to quote from material in the collections of the Vassar College Library.

Charles Scribner's Sons Books for Young Readers
Macmillan Publishing Company, 866 Third Avenue, New York, NY 10022
Collier Macmillan Canada, Inc.

Printed in the United States of America
First Edition   10 9 8 7 6 5 4 3 2 1

Library of Congress Cataloging-in-Publication Data
Hodges, Margaret.   Making a difference: the story of an American family
Margaret Hodges. — 1st ed.   p.   cm.
Summary: Traces the lives and accomplishments of the extraordinary Mary Sherwood and her five children, who played an important part in bringing great changes in higher education and voting rights for women, opportunities for government service, and awareness of the need to preserve the country's natural wonders.
1. Sherwood family—Juvenile literature. 2. Roosevelt, Eleanor,
1884–1962—Friends and associates—Juvenile literature.
3. United States—Biography—Juvenile literature. [1. Sherwood family.
2. Roosevelt, Eleanor, 1884–1962—Friends and associates.
3. United States—Biography.]   I. Title.
CT274.S533H63   1989   973.91′092′2—dc19   88–31131
[B]   [920]   CIP   AC   ISBN 0–684–18979–8

To the Sherwoods
and to all who have helped me tell their story

CONTENTS

... World-losers and world-forsakers,
On whom the pale moon gleams:
Yet we are the movers and shakers
Of the world forever, it seems.

—Arthur William
Edgar O'Shaughnessy
(1844–1881)

FOREWORD

Happiness is a mysterious thing. Whatever it is, some people have it, no matter how much trouble they meet along the way. It belongs especially to people who believe that they can do what they set out to do and, as a result, accomplish miracles. The Sherwood family were like that—Mary and her children: Margaret, Helen, Jean, Penelope, and Sidney, Jr.

They thought of themselves as ordinary people, and certainly they were not rich or famous or powerful. But ordinary people can do extraordinary things. From their old farmhouse at Cornwall, New York, on the Hudson River, the Sherwoods moved into the wider life that flowed along the Hudson River valley and beyond. Perhaps they themselves did not guess how much they would accomplish.

Not that the Sherwoods were unappreciated in their lifetimes. Long before Franklin D. Roosevelt became president of the United States, the Sherwoods were linked to the Roosevelt family of the great house at Hyde Park twenty-five miles up the Hudson from Cornwall. When the Roosevelts moved to the White House, the Sherwoods often wrote to Franklin or Eleanor Roosevelt for help, always in some good cause, and help usually came, from that most powerful of families. The Roosevelts, "movers and shakers of the world," did not forget the old friendship, and the consequences of that friendship are being enjoyed today by a generation of Americans who never heard of the Sherwoods. During the century that began with the Civil War, this family played a part in bringing about great changes in American lives: higher education and voting rights for women, pioneer work for women as physicians, new opportunities for government service, new awareness of our need to preserve the natural wonders of "America the Beautiful." It all began with Mary Sherwood.

❖ 1 ❖

MARY

President Roosevelt once said, "Oh, Sidney is a fine boy, but you ought to meet his mother." And Eleanor Roosevelt said that every time she got discouraged, she would telephone Mary Sherwood to ask if she might drive down to the little house on the hill at Cornwall for tea. "Mrs. Sherwood always cheers me up," she said. "She is always looking ahead." On New Year's Eve, 1940, when Sidney, Jr., was having dinner at the White House, he remarked to Granny Roosevelt, the president's mother, that she and his own mother had faced somewhat the same challenge: Both had lost their husbands and had to face a parent's responsibilities alone. Granny Roosevelt answered, "There was no comparison. I had everything I needed, ample income and plenty of help. My task was relatively easy. What she did was a miracle."

The miracle that Mary Sherwood performed began with her childhood in the simple house at the top of the hill above Cornwall, New York, a small town between West Point and

Newburgh. It is a town of no special importance, although the lower part, known as Cornwall-on-Hudson, has a spectacular view of the great river. As the main street climbs the hill, Cornwall-on-Hudson becomes plain Cornwall, and the street winds upward into Angola Road. The Sherwoods lived at 51 Angola Road. Mary Sherwood lived there all her life, except for a few short years in Baltimore with her husband, Sidney Sherwood, Sr.

Mary's father, Dr. William Beattie, had bought the house in 1854 and moved in with his young wife, Mary Jane, and their baby boy, Frank. The place had a homey, hospitable look. It was a story and a half high and was painted white, with green shutters. There were eight rooms. William and Mary Jane slept in the first-floor bedroom that faced the road across the lawn where William planted maple trees. At the back of the house he planted an elm that grew to be twice the height of the house. Past the elm was the big red barn and a slope down to a peaceful meadow where Idlewild Brook widened into a pond. Beyond the brook the woods began, climbing to the top of three peaks: Deer Hill, Black Rock, and Storm King. This was the view from the library, which also served as William's office. The kitchen–dining room, too, looked toward the hills from the south windows, and there was a porch at the back of the house where William and Mary Jane could enjoy their view at the end of long, hot summer days, William smoking and talking about the problems of the patients whom he had visited in many miles of driving since early morning. Mary Jane would knit while the light lasted.

William Beattie had been one of seven children, living on a farm at the village of Coldenham, a few miles northwest of Cornwall. Grandfather Beattie wanted all the boys to go to college so that they could become Presbyterian ministers.

The Angola Road house in winter

Hezekiah, David, and William all attended Union College in Schenectady, and Hezekiah and David did go on to study for the ministry as their father had planned. But William obstinately refused, whereupon his father handed him ten dollars and told him to expect no more help toward an education.

William bought a ticket for Philadelphia and stayed with family friends while he worked at any jobs he could find and saved his money. Then he heard of a little school at Darby, Louisiana, that needed a teacher. He applied and was accepted. Traveling by train and Mississippi River steamboat, he reached New Orleans and made his way to Darby, where he taught until the following spring. He had earned $126.63 for his winter's work. He was hoping to do better the following year when he met a wealthy planter, a Captain Barrow, who was looking for a man to work in his sugar business. He hired William, offering him fifty dollars a month. In six months William had made such a good impression that Captain Barrow asked him to tutor his three sons. William Beattie became part of the Barrows' family life, enjoying the hunt and the great dinners that spread out to the long veranda on warm summer evenings. His own family's strict puritanical habits forbade dancing, but in Louisiana William danced.

At the end of two years with the Barrow boys he returned to the North to study medicine and went to board with his brother Hezekiah, who was now a minister. An energetic and serious young man, William earned his M.D. degree and the admiration of his family and northern friends. He was not only handsome but sophisticated, and when he walked up the aisle of his brother's church one Sunday morning, he caused a stir. That morning Mary Jane Sherwood saw him for the first time. After the church service they met and fell in love at once. Mary Jane was still in her teens, but she had had a good education at a seminary for girls in Saratoga, and she had already taught school for three years; she was old enough to know her own mind. Before long, they were married.

William heard that a country doctor was needed in the mountains along the Hudson between Newburgh and West Point. Settling at Cornwall, he soon became the much-loved doctor for many isolated families. Though he worked long hours, six days a week, he never got rich. The town paid him twenty-five dollars a year to take care of Cornwall families who were too poor to pay, but he never turned away patients who could not pay, no matter where they lived. The first year, he rode over a thousand miles by horse and buggy or sleigh.

During their first ten years of marriage, William and Mary

Jane lived through not only the stress of the Civil War but
personal sorrows as well. Their first child, Frank, was timid
but very bright, his parents' pride and joy. Another little
boy, Alson, lived only a few days. Then came Rosa, a pretty,
gifted child, and Lee, a handsome boy who very early began
to take responsibility in solving family problems. When the
next child, Matthew, was born, Frank was seven and already
able to read and write. One day, when he had been playing
in the barn with Rosa, William's chore boy persuaded Frank
to climb to the highest haymow. Afraid, but not wanting to
be called a coward, Frank climbed, lost his footing, and fell
twenty feet to the barn floor, striking his head. Rosa ran to
the house, screaming, "Ma, Ma! Frankie is dead!" Mary
Jane rushed to the barn just as William drove into it from his
day's work. He carried Frank to the house, where the little
boy lay unconscious for four days. At last he began to rally
physically, and he did not forget what he had learned before
the accident, but mentally he stopped growing. He learned
no more from books.

In 1864 the Civil War was still raging, but life was relatively normal in the little house on the hill, and Mary Jane
was expecting another baby. On a blustery spring morning in
March she was sitting on the sofa by the kitchen stove, helping her children to dress. Thirza Brooks, who lived in the
house as a "mother's helper," was cooking breakfast when
Mary Jane felt the first birth pangs. Thirza sent the children
out of the kitchen and called William, who delivered the
baby on the sofa.

He carried his wife upstairs and made her comfortable in
the big guest room, where a fire was burning in the coal
stove. Thirza followed with the baby, saying that it was the
homeliest one she had ever seen. She then gave the other
children their breakfast. Ten-year-old Frank was sent to ask

a kind neighbor to give the new baby, Mary Abigail, her first bath, while William drove off to bring another neighbor, a practical nurse, to take care of both mother and child. Mary Jane was too weak to nurse the baby and wondered how long this scrawny child could live on the various substitutes for mother's milk that she tried. Finally, Thirza Brooks advised adding a teaspoon of cream to the baby's food several times a day. Whether this was the reason or not, Mary Abigail was soon growing normally and was taking her first steps by the time she was a year old.

As she grew, Mary turned into what grown-ups called "a handful." Her mother often had to say, "Mary, speak more softly. . . . Gently, Mary, gently," or, when she had been especially troublesome, "Mary Abigail, you *must* not . . ." But her father called her Puss and would come to her defense when she had been scolded, saying, "After all, she is a good child."

Mary had every intention of being "a good child," but growing up as the youngest in the family had its problems. Her parents taught her to tell the truth; her brothers and sisters told her not to be a tattletale. Grown-ups praised her when she learned to read at the age of four; other children would burst into tears or tease and torment her if their parents said, "Mary Beattie is only four and she can read. You could learn, too, if you would try."

Meanwhile, Mary learned some long words that her mother used about her. Being "obstinate" meant not doing as you were told. Being "boisterous" meant shouting at the top of your lungs and jumping up and down on the sofa. Once when she was playing with her dolls, she heard her mother say to a visitor, "Well, Rosa has a very keen sense of propriety, something that Mary seems to lack." In time she learned what propriety meant: sitting quietly while grown-ups talked, crossing your legs at the ankles and folding your hands in your lap when there were visitors, not saying everything that came into your head, even if it was true, not looking too pleased that you could read when you were four years old and knew some eight-year-olds who could not.

It was so easy to read. Mary had learned just by climbing into her father's lap when he was reading the evening newspaper. He was six feet tall and weighed two hundred and forty pounds. His stomach made a comfortable pillow for her head while she looked at words in the newspaper and asked question after question. He always answered patiently, remembering his days as a schoolteacher. Since Mary Jane too had taught school, they decided to go on teaching their children at home, feeling sure that they could do a better job than the little school in Cornwall.

William assigned the children's lessons every evening and heard them recite the following afternoon. Each child had morning chores to do—that, too, was an important part of education—but Mary Jane saw to it that there was plenty of time to study after chores were finished. She gave each child her personal attention, with help over the hard spots, especially for Frank. She was always cheerful and had a way of controlling her family without giving many orders.

By the time chores were done and lessons learned, William had come home for the noonday dinner and a nap on the old sofa. Mary would climb up and over him, curling down for her own nap in the space behind his knees. After the nap, Pa heard his children recite, corrected their mistakes, and sent them off to play, before he himself drove away on another round of house calls or saw patients in the library-office.

Only one day in the week was different. Sunday, the Sabbath, was strictly kept in the old Scotch-Irish Covenanter tradition of the Presbyterian Church. On Sunday mornings the Beattie children walked down to Cornwall-on-Hudson, two miles away, to arrive before nine-thirty, when Sunday school began. Later, Pa and Ma would drive to church with the team of horses and two-seated wagon. The children stayed on with them for the eleven o'clock service, filling a whole pew. During the long prayer, Mary usually fell asleep with her head on her mother's lap, waking up in time to put her penny in the collection plate.

After church came the drive home and a wonderful Sunday noon dinner. But the holy day was far from over. In the afternoon, Father put the big Bible on the kitchen table beside another great heavy book, a concordance, in which every Bible word was listed alphabetically and located by Bible chapter and verse. Father would give a word, such as *love,* and the children would spend the afternoon finding and copying out all the Bible verses where *love* could be found. No one went for a walk or a ride or a visit on Sunday. Father would see a patient, but not a visitor. When Mother had Sunday visitors, Father would retreat to the barn, looking displeased.

After Sunday supper, if no patients came, the children showed Father the Bible verses they had found, and he gave them an examination in the catechism, the list of religious questions that every Covenanter child had to answer. It began: "What is the chief end of man?" Mary had no idea what this meant, but she knew the answer: "Man's chief end is to glorify God and to enjoy Him forever." Having got it right, it was her turn to ask the next question. So it went, questions and answers following each other like a game, until in time the Beattie children knew the entire catechism by heart. Years later, Mary still remembered it, word for word. Yet, as she grew older, some of the catechism was impossible to accept: "What are you by nature?" "I am by nature an enemy of God and an heir of Hell." No. She could not believe it. She also learned at church and at home that God was a loving Father, and that she did believe.

The week before Christmas when she was four years old, her father bought her a pair of ice skates as an early present from Santa, who wanted her to be able to skate with Rosa and the boys on Christmas morning. Until now, Mary had been satisfied to sit on a big log at the edge of the pond, to watch the others skating, sometimes to see a deer in the woods. But today the pond was a whole new world. The boys helped her tie her skates on and started her off on her first wobbling steps across the ice. Sliding, falling, getting up to try again in spite of bumps and bruises, Mary loved all of it.

When Christmas morning came, she was ready. Father and the children packed themselves with two young friends into the big sleigh, the bells jingling on the horse's harness as they drove down to the Hudson. The ice was like glass and about three feet thick, so strong that a few other young people were driving on it to Newburgh with horse and cutter. The Beatties skated all morning long and never tired. Skating was to be one of Mary's joys until she was eighty-five years old.

Another memory of winter was so vivid that she could describe every detail many years later for her own children:

Father traveled on horseback or in a two-wheeled sulky over miles of rough mountain roads to reach needy families. In the winter of 1868, when I was four years old, he was called to Ike O'Dell's cabin, five miles back in the mountains. Ike's job was hauling cordwood to the brick yards near Newburgh. He had the habit of stopping at the taverns on his way home. One day he drank too much and about a mile from his home fell asleep in his wagon. His horses ran away, throwing him into an icy ditch, and one of his legs was broken in the fall. When his family saw the horses coming with the empty wagon, his two big boys took their sled and went to look for Ike. They found him almost unconscious and brought him back to the cabin. Then they came for my father, who went with them and set the broken leg.

The next day Father said that I might go up there with him for a sleigh ride. It was midwinter. The snow was deep and the air clear and cold. Mother packed a big basket of food for the O'Dells and bundled me up in my woolly coat, hood, and mittens. With a hot brick to keep my feet warm, I cuddled down under the buffalo robe, close to Father. He was wearing his heavy coat with a cape and high beaver collar, and his fur cap and mittens. I keenly remember my delight in the jingle of sleigh bells as I watched the snow sparkling like little diamonds in the glorious sunshine.

We began climbing Mount Rascal and soon afterward saw the smoke from the chimney of Ike's cabin. Father tied the horse to a tree and covered her with a blanket. Then he carried me into the cabin. There was one room with a stove, table, three long benches, and three beds, all as neat and warm as possible. There were four children, one being a little barefooted girl of my age. Mrs. O'Dell unpacked the basket of food my mother had sent while my father made Ike more comfortable. Then he bundled me up and we said goodbye. I fell asleep with Father's strong arm around me and did not wake until he had carried me into our cozy kitchen and dropped me on the sofa.

Everyone knew Dr. Beattie's cutter sleigh by sight. He answered calls that often meant hours of driving on rough roads in freezing weather, for little or no pay. Giving service was part of the creed William Beattie lived by and part of the heritage he left to his children. He did not have much else to leave.

The following summer, when Mary was five, William took the whole family to New York City by steamboat. Mary had seen steamboats many times, but to be a passenger herself was thrilling. With a picnic lunch the Beatties boarded the *Mary Powell*, the smartest and fastest boat on the Hudson. William Beattie pointed out the great crag that rose above the west bank of the wide, calm river. This was the face of Storm King, the old mountain friend whose back Mary saw every day from the windows at home. How grand and noble it was, the Beatties' own Storm King! In 1869 no one could have guessed that the beauty of Storm King would one day be threatened and that Mary Beattie Sherwood's children would rise up to help save it.

When the *Mary Powell* docked at New York City, a horse-drawn streetcar took the Beatties to Central Park and its wonderful new zoo, where the monkeys were the chief attraction. The return trip included a stop downtown to see Cooper Union, the free school recently founded by Peter Cooper, the great American inventor, builder of *Tom Thumb*, the first practical American-built locomotive. Peter Cooper was a leader in New York City and was working hard to establish a public school system. He believed that ordinary working people must have a good education, and Cooper Union offered just that, a chance for young men and women with jobs to go to school at night, their only free time.

On the very day when the Beatties visited the Union, Peter Cooper himself, now an elderly man, was there, posing for a bust being made by a sculptor. With her glimpse of Peter Cooper and his school, Mary had unconsciously taken in the idea that education in a school, a real school, was a great and wonderful thing. A seed had been planted; it would grow.

Meanwhile, play was the most important thing in the

world. It went on for Mary most of the day and into the long summer evenings. Her father and mother welcomed the young neighbors who came to play hide-and-seek or to carry on wild water fights until dark. Mary was always in the thick of it. The big old barn, the shop, wheelbarrow house, henhouse, woodshed, pigpen, and twelve acres of land made a perfect playground for a child who was more tomboy than angel.

But Mary's boisterous energy was hard on her mother and she heard things she was not meant to hear. It might be a neighbor saying, "Mary Jane Beattie hasn't been really well since that last child was born." Or, "It's a pity that little girl is such a handful. Her mother never gets a chance to rest." For whatever reason, by the time she was ten, Mary had noticed that her mother stayed at home when Pa took the children for overnight camping trips.

The wildest and most beautiful lake in the mountains near Cornwall was Sutherland's Pond. Pa made a big flat-bottomed boat to fit on the running gear of the lumber wagon in place of the regular wagon box. Loading the boat with hay for the horses, a tent, blankets, fishing tackle, and clothes basket, the children would drive off with William for two days and a night at Sutherland's Pond. Only Mary Jane stayed behind, insisting that she was never lonely and that she was happy when she knew they were happy.

All the Beattie children learned to handle horses. Mary already could ride well, wearing one of her mother's long skirts and using Rosa's sidesaddle. Now on the camping trips she learned to drive the two horses that pulled the wagon. On the steepest part of the mountain road to Sutherland's Pond, Father gave her the reins, while he and the others walked to lighten the load.

Their destination was one end of the pond where pitcher

plants and pond lilies grew in profusion and the air was fragrant. The boys gathered wood, pitched the tent, and fed the horses. Father went fishing. Rosa and Mary cooked supper over the campfire. Afterward they sat around the fire until bedtime, unless it rained, and slept wrapped in their blankets on the hay. They were up at dawn to make the most of every moment in camp. Father and the boys fished while Rosa sketched. Mary built playhouses, paddled in the water, and hunted for wildflowers. The day was never long enough.

When they came home, Mary Jane was always glad to see them but said cheerfully that their two days had given her a chance to catch up on her work. She had a household helper, a woman who came up from Cornwall, and the children were learning to help, but even so, there was a lot to do: cleaning, washing, ironing, cooking, baking, churning, caring for the chickens, and weeding the garden. Mary Jane made her own clothes and dresses for the girls. She made the boys' shirts and taught Rosa and Mary to sew. Since she never complained, the family took her busy days for granted, and it was only by chance that Mary heard her mother speak of a slight curvature of the spine that made her back painful much of the time. She began to wonder whether her mother's responsibilities had been already too great for her strength when Mary was born. Should she have been born? On the heels of this thought came a determination to help her mother in every possible way.

Her mother was soon to need help, more than ever. By the time Mary was ten, Frank was a grown man. He had fine instincts, but when he earned a little money on occasional jobs in the town, he would follow other men into the taverns that lined the main street. A very little alcohol made him drunk, and he acquired a craving for it. From that time on, home life in the Beatties' house was changed. Mary Jane no longer invited guests, not knowing when or how Frank might appear. For Mary it was as if her childhood had closed.

Another change in family life came when Rosa and Lee went away to school. Rosa went to Elmira Female College, far away in central New York State. Lee was only twenty miles away at Middletown, where he lived with Uncle Asher and attended a good high school to prepare for college, but he, too, left a gap in the family circle and was missed. Frank, Matt, and Mary were left at home, studying with Father.

Mary begged him to allow her to go to the little public school in Cornwall where some of her friends went, and to make her happy, William finally agreed to let her enroll for the spring term. He doubted that she would learn much. At seven and a half, she had already read the Bible from beginning to end, and now she was far ahead of other children of her age. As expected, she did not fit into the curriculum either of that school or of a private school that had just been opened by a retired minister.

William once more took Mary's schooling into his own hands, adding Latin and Greek to her other studies. In between lessons, she loved to ride. There were always at least two horses stabled in the barn, and Mary had her father's balky horse, Charlie, for her own use. She went off for long rides into the mountains, carrying the New Testament in Greek in her sidesaddle pocket. When Charlie balked, she often had time to translate a verse or two before he was ready to start on.

Rosa, Lee, and Matt had all gone away to school when their father was struck down with typhoid fever, perhaps brought on by drinking water from a contaminated well. There was no effective treatment for typhoid fever; one either lived through it or died of it. William was desperately ill. Mary Jane nursed him day and night, with only occasional help from kind neighbors. When her husband was recovering, she collapsed as a result of fatigue. Mary was terrified. Suddenly she realized what it would mean to lose her parents, and, young as she was, she nursed her mother through her illness.

That year she was often alone and had to find ways to entertain herself, using all that she had learned from doing chores or seeing them done. Now that she could sew, she designed and made a whole toy trunkful of doll clothes, and she built playhouses. When her brothers came home in the summer, they helped her fasten a platform in the crotch of a large cherry tree and made a little ladder to reach it. Mary read and napped in the cherry tree. She had learned how to make her own happiness, without spending money.

Rosa left Elmira College at the end of her junior year and came home to Cornwall. During her last term she had had an attack of pleurisy that left her with a cough. William adored Rosa. When he made calls on horseback, she often went with him. She loved art and music, she loved life and people; she was attractive in every way and the picture of health. Her father refused to believe there could be anything seriously wrong with her now, and he liked having her at home. The little cough was noticeable only in the mornings. She went on with her landscape drawing, painting, and music and took over Mary's lessons, which now included French. In the spring a classmate from Elmira College told Rosa about a little district school in Vermont where a teacher was needed. Rosa applied and was accepted, but soon she found the work tiring. Her cough was getting worse. Her father went immediately and brought Rosa home, but tuberculosis had developed. In August Rosa died.

William never forgave himself for refusing to believe that Rosa was already ill when she went to Vermont. From this time on, Mary's health was a constant worry to him, and his anxiety became a handicap in her education. He fully intended that she should go to college, as she wanted very much to do, but if she had even a slight cold, he would take her out of school and keep her at home for the rest of the semester. She went on with Greek and Latin under his guidance.

Lee was now at Princeton Theological Seminary, studying for the ministry, and decided to take a year off to earn some money. He got a job at a small preparatory school for boys in New Jersey and arranged for Mary to attend as the only girl student. Since her brother was on the staff and could watch over her health, her father was willing for her to go. She was fifteen years old and had sixteen boys as classmates. There were picnics, skating parties, hikes, and sleigh rides. A big box sleigh would be filled with straw, buffalo robes, and hot bricks to warm cold feet on long rides. The students came back to school after nightfall, singing to the sound of jingling bells as the strong horses trotted over the packed snow. There was always a stop at a roadside hotel for sandwiches and hot cocoa. Without the approval of the school, the boys taught Mary to jump a three-foot fence and to play football. It was a blissfully happy winter.

The next winter Mary was again at home with her father and mother, studying, riding horseback, and beginning to take part in Sunday school and missionary work for the Presbyterian church. Another happiness was to find some teenage girls who wanted to do interesting things together. Mary was the founder and president of Cornwall's Agassiz Society, named for Louis Agassiz, a Swiss zoologist and geologist who had taught at Harvard and inspired a whole generation of Americans to study directly from nature. Mary's Agassiz Society of sixteen girls took long weekly hikes in the mountains—"our mountains," she called them—and collected more than a hundred specimens of rock, which they analyzed and labeled. The collection was stored, probably in the old barn, at 51 Angola Road.

Mary needed one more year of schooling before entering college and had chosen Smith College at Northampton, Massachusetts. To prepare for this, her father allowed her to attend Schenectady Collegiate Institute, where she would live with family friends. All went well until the day before graduation when the principal asked Mary whether she had passed her algebra examination for college entrance. The school records were sketchy.

"I finished algebra last year under my brother Lee's teaching," Mary answered.

Professor Halsen was not satisfied. "You say you have passed your algebra, but how do I know you have?" he demanded.

Mary's old untamed hot temper rose. "Have I recited to you for a whole year, and you don't know whether or not I would tell a lie?" she answered furiously. She ran out of the room, slamming the door.

The next day Professor Halsen sent a teacher to tell her that if she would apologize for her behavior, she would receive her diploma; otherwise, she would not.

Obstinate as ever, Mary would not apologize.

The graduation exercises took place in a crowded church. Each member of the senior class was called to the platform to receive her diploma, except Mary. She sat alone in the front pew, feeling a hundred pairs of eyes staring at her. Professor Halsen kept her diploma. That was the nearest she ever came to owning one, and the school in Schenectady was the last one she ever attended.

Sometimes Mary felt angry and resentful. Her brothers had attended college and gone on to useful careers, Matt as a doctor in New York City, Lee as a minister. Rosa had gone to college and had become a teacher. Only Frank, poor Frank, and Mary, it seemed, were to spend their lives at home. Her father must have understood her feelings, because he took her at the age of twenty for a winter in New Orleans. He had kept his old southern friendships, and Mary had a season of dancing and roller skating, of laughing and flirting with boys. They stayed on through the parties and dazzling parades of Mardi Gras and topped off the New Orleans fun with some hunting and fishing in Texas. They reached Washington on March 4, 1885, the day of Grover Cleveland's inauguration as president of the United States, and were in the great crowd that watched him take the oath of office. William Beattie had been born and brought up as a Democrat; there had not been a Democratic president for twenty-four years. Mary caught her father's enthusiasm and wished she could have helped to put President Cleveland in office. She had just passed her twenty-first birthday, but because she was a woman, she would never be able to vote.

Yet that "never" was already being challenged in upstate New York. As long ago as 1848, two valiant women, Elizabeth Cady Stanton and Lucretia Coffin Mott, both of them as obstinate as Mary Beattie, had organized at Seneca Falls, New York, the first national convention on women's rights. Mrs. Mott's husband, James Mott, presided at the convention, and other men, too, were sympathetic to the cause, but the vote for women remained a faint hope. Generally speaking, most men and many women disapproved of the idea.

When Mary and her father reached home from New Orleans, nothing had changed. Every day had its quiet duties, and horizons shrank again to the limits of Cornwall.

Mary made one more try for college. At best, her education had been sketchy—in and out of seven different schools, for a total of only three and a half years, with her father as tutor at the end of each interrupted semester—but she took the entrance examination for Mount Holyoke College in Massachusetts, where there were good opportunities to earn part of the expenses. Mary passed the examination, and her mother was willing for her to go, but once again, as so many times before, her father felt anxious about her leaving home. He could not throw off his old sense of guilt over Rosa's death. On a visit to her Sherwood relatives at Ballston Spa in upstate New York, Mary had a long talk about the college question with her Uncle Thomas, her mother's brother. He spoke about the heavy burden her mother carried, never complaining about her painful back or about her constant care of Frank. As long as Mary had known her parents, they had set examples of helping others. She decided to give up going to college, but she was bitterly disappointed.

When she went home to Cornwall, she thought of what she was losing: a wider world, learning, new friendships. She realized more than ever what it meant to live with an alcoholic. Frank might be at home, puttering about the house, often singing old Salvation Army songs. But if there was silence, and Frank could not be found, someone had to walk down to Cornwall and bring him home from a saloon. Mary took on that humiliating task.

Still, joy kept breaking through the sadness. Douglas Pierson, her next-door neighbor since early childhood, laid out a tennis court on the Pierson property, and Mary learned to play so well that she was always wanted for a game. Boys liked her, and there were plenty of boys at the tennis court. Mary made a scarlet jacket and black wool skirt that every boy in the neighborhood noticed. And when autumn came, rides into the hills were more wonderful than ever, the red swamp maple bright on the mountain slopes, her horse's feet rustling through leaves that fell thicker with every gust of wind, the sweet smell of wood smoke from farmhouse chimneys, and at the end of the ride the lantern light on the warm dark beams above the horse stalls in the home stable.

Quite unexpectedly came the greatest joy of Mary's life. She fell in love with Sidney Sherwood, one of a large family of her cousins at Ballston Spa. Mary had known Sidney always, but in recent years she had not seen much of him and was rather in awe of him. He was four years older than she was, a serious, thoughtful young man, handsome, a brilliant student who had graduated from Princeton in 1879, when he was only nineteen years old. Woodrow Wilson, later to be president of the United States, was a member of that class and was Sidney's close friend. After college, Sidney had traveled in Europe for two years with a retired minister who had many scholarly friends. They opened up the Old World of learning and culture to young Sidney. By 1887 he had graduated from Columbia Law School and soon established himself as partner of a judge on Wall Street in New York City. No wonder Mary Beattie was impressed.

Sidney's family all seemed brilliant to Mary. One sister, Belle, had graduated from Elmira College and gone with her husband to Persia as a missionary. Together they were translating the New Testament into Persian. Another sister, Mary, had graduated from Vassar College and was studying medicine in Zurich. The youngest sister, Margaret, was also a Vassar graduate, now studying abroad and planning to write and teach. By comparison with these admirable sisters of Sidney's, Mary Beattie felt like a country bumpkin. She did not expect Sidney Sherwood to think twice about her. With her erratic education and her impulsive, boisterous, obstinate nature, what would he ever see in her?

Mary's brother Matt, practicing medicine in New York City, was going to be married in the fall of 1887 and had rented a small apartment on West Fifty-first Street. He asked Mary to keep house for him during the summer. Her father and mother thought that she should go, and a glorious summer began. A client of Sidney's owned a little shack on the south shore of Long Island, a mile from any house. Sidney and Matt rented the shack for the summer and furnished it enough for weekend camping parties. Everyone lived in bathing suits and cooked outdoors over beachwood fires. Mary was the girl Sidney chose every day for races on the sand or swimming in the surf. At night, when they sat around the fire, listening to the waves and talking, or singing, Sidney always found a place beside Mary. By the end of the summer, Sidney had fallen as deeply in love with Mary as she already was with him. They announced their engagement, and Mary wanted to be married at once.

But Sidney had come to a turning point in his career. His law practice in New York City had shown him how corrupt politics could be. The system of bossism was in full sway, power being held by cynical men who bought and sold influence, jobs, and votes. Men of high principles, thoroughly trained in government, were needed. Sidney decided to leave his law practice and go to Baltimore, where he could earn a doctor's degree in history and political science at

Sidney and Mary Sherwood

Johns Hopkins University. For at least two years he would have no money to spend on getting married and setting up a household.

To Mary the delay seemed unbearable. Impulsive as always, she considered running away from the problem by going overseas as a missionary like Sidney's sister Belle. The church was asking for missionaries to go to Korea. On the other side of the world she might be able to get Sidney out of her mind. Besides, she would be doing public service, as he wanted to do. Fortunately, a wise old minister persuaded her not to follow such an emotional impulse. He advised her to stay at home where she was needed and to be patient; the two years would pass.

But there were objections to the match. According to some strong opinions in both the Sherwood and the Beattie families, first cousins should not marry. Sidney and Mary were double first cousins; Sidney's father, Thomas Sherwood, had married a Beattie, and Mary's mother was

Thomas's sister. She, too, had married a Beattie. The relationship was too close. In the closely knit Sherwood-Beattie clans, arguments, even quarrels flared up over the question of Mary and Sidney's marriage. It was against biblical law, according to the teaching of the Covenanter church. And some of the relatives opposed the marriage for medical reasons; there was a theory that children of double first cousins might be abnormal. Mary was in despair. Was duty once again going to come between her and her dearest wish? Her father and mother approved of the marriage after an eminent doctor told them that there was no medical reason to fear one more marriage between two families as healthy as the Sherwoods and the Beatties. Mary's much loved and respected brother Lee, the minister, was still bitterly opposed, but as the two years passed, family objection died down, Sidney got his Ph.D., and the day for the wedding was set.

On September 3, 1891, Mary and Sidney were to be married under the trees on the front lawn at Cornwall. Sidney's missionary sister, Belle, had come from Persia with her missionary husband, bringing a beautiful rug on which the bride and groom would stand. Eighty friends and relatives were arriving, including eight dignified Presbyterian ministers. One of them, Mary's uncle, would perform the long and solemn service. All of them would have been surprised and disturbed if they had known how far Mary had strayed in her thinking from the strict and severe beliefs of her ancestral church. She now felt sure of almost nothing except the loving fatherhood of God and her own blissful happiness in loving Sidney.

By the night before the wedding the nervous tension was too much, and Mary and Sidney thought of eloping to get away from the strain. But eloping would be unfair to the family who had come to take part in the celebration, and especially unfair to the nearest and dearest ones who had worked hard to make every detail perfect for the ceremony and the banquet that was to follow. Most of all, an elopement would hurt Mary Jane, the mother of the bride. So the wedding took place as planned. As soon as possible after the banquet, Mary and Sidney made their escape to honeymoon at Magnolia, one of the loveliest spots on the rugged coast of Massachusetts. Suddenly, life seemed too beautiful to be real.

Sidney had an offer to begin teaching finance at the University of Pennsylvania, but first he wanted to take Mary to Paris and to Italy. He himself had had two years abroad; now Mary should have her chance to travel. She was tempted, having spent her whole life at home. But she had always been taught not to yield to temptation. And wasn't it enough to have the perfect happiness of being Sidney's wife? She persuaded him to put off the trip he had planned. They enjoyed their summer at Cornwall and Ballston Spa, and there would be plenty of chances to go abroad later.

But there were no chances to go later. Almost immediately, Sidney had a flattering offer from Johns Hopkins University at Baltimore in a graduate school so prestigious that he could not say no. He was to take the place of a leading scholar, a professor of political economy, who was retiring. Mary was thrilled that Sidney should be honored, and they moved to Baltimore. Shortly afterward, their first baby, Margaret, was born. During the next nine years came four more children: Helen, Jean, Penelope, and Sidney, Jr., whom Mary proudly named for his father. Life was too busy for more talk of European travel. Mary and Sidney bought a house for their growing family at 412 Hawthorn Road in

Roland Park, a wooded suburb of Baltimore. Mary took care of the children with the help of a cook and a nursemaid; she entertained students and a brilliant circle of friends. When Woodrow Wilson gave a course in international law at Johns Hopkins, he brought his wife to visit the Sherwoods. He was an ardent Democrat and Sidney a Republican, but they renewed their old college friendship.

Mary helped to organize a club for four hundred women, who took part in all the cultural interests of Baltimore. They attended the opera and heard lectures on art, music, literature, and civics. They brought famous speakers to Baltimore. For Mary it was almost like going to college.

While her mind was being nourished in the atmosphere of university life, Mary's love of the outdoors was as strong as ever. Everyone was bicycling; she rode with Sidney for miles along country roads. One afternoon, about five miles from home, at a green field, they passed four men hitting white balls with long-handled clubs. Golf was a new game in the United States; Mary and Sidney had never seen it played. The next day Sidney bought some clubs, golf balls, and a book of rules. A friend who was an engineer helped him lay out a putting green in a field near Roland Park, and this grew in time to be the eighteen-hole golf course of the Baltimore Country Club, founded by Sidney and some of his friends. Their wives were charter members, and golf became a passion for Mary as well as for Sidney.

In the summers, when they took the children back to Cornwall to visit their Beattie grandparents, one more pleasure was added to a life that was already perfect. In 1894 new links opened, and Sidney and Mary joined the Storm King Golf Club. Their hours together on the golf course were treasured.

Then in quick succession came sad changes at Cornwall,

cutting all the old home ties. Mary's brother Frank died of pneumonia, and their mother, taking care of Frank to the last, died of the same disease a week later. Dr. Beattie stayed on in the Cornwall house for another year with his friend and neighbor, Douglas Pierson's father, for company. The two old men kept house together until 1899, when William died of a heart attack.

For the first time, 51 Angola Road stood vacant. Knowing what Cornwall meant to Mary, her brother Matt bought the farm and gave Mary the house. She and Sidney looked forward to using the house in the summers. They had running water installed and built a longer porch that faced the mountains.

But Roland Park was home now for Mary. In spite of her sorrow over the loss of her parents and her brother, her Baltimore life was ideally happy. Sidney was writing textbooks on political economy; he was making speeches at important meetings. His reputation was growing, and he was giving public service as he had dreamed of doing, helping to improve standards for American business. Mackenzie King, later prime minister of Canada, applied for a fellowship to take a course under Sidney Sherwood. Theodore Marburg, an American diplomat, took one of Sidney's courses.

Sidney and Mary had always hoped to have a son and were delighted when Sidney, Jr., was born in the spring of 1901. In June Mary took the five children to Cornwall. Sidney went to Ballston Spa for a few days to visit his mother, who was old and ill. With them were Sidney's sister, Dr. Mary Sherwood, her partner, Dr. Lilian Welsh, and a nurse. Sidney was about to return to Cornwall when he had a slight accident, cutting his thumb as he pruned some young trees in the orchard. Blood poisoning developed. An-

The Sherwood girls in 1899

tibiotics were unknown. Dr. Mary wrote a reassuring note to Cornwall, however, and said that another doctor had been called in for consultation. Then came a telegram. Mary went at once to Ballston Spa.

Years later she wrote for her children an account of Sidney's death. "He asked me not to let the others see me grieve, adding, 'How can I leave you without more provision? You had better sell the Roland Park house, stay in Cornwall for a year, and then do what seems best for you. Sit up and face it, darling, sweetheart, light of my life. I love you. I love you. I love you.' And he was gone."

"Sit up and face it." In her journal, Mary followed Sidney's well-remembered words with Emily Dickinson's poem:

> My life closed twice before its close—
> It yet remains to see
> If Immortality unveil
> A third event to me

The five Sherwood children on the lawn at Cornwall in the summer of 1901

Mary two years after Sidney's death

So huge, so hopeless to conceive
As these that twice befell.
Parting is all we know of heaven,
And all we need of hell.

After these lines Mary wrote: "The ending of my childhood closed the first door. Then dawned the glorious day:
love, marriage, companionship, home, children, social and
international interests, health, complete happiness. That

door closed. . . . I could not understand, I have never understood, how the great Power I had ever thought was a loving Father, could permit one of His children to be taken to the pinnacle of happiness, then thrown on its face and expect it to rise and walk! I was stunned, could only repeat over and over, 'How could He permit it?' I could not pray. God was no longer a loving Father but a cruel Power."

❖ 2 ❖

GRETCHEN—
AND MARGARET MERRIAM

This is Gretchen's story, and the story of how she became the writer, Merriam Sherwood.

When parents name a baby after a special person, they seem to think that the name has a mysterious power, as if it could somehow influence the child. Sidney Sherwood, Sr., had been named for the gallant Sir Philip Sidney; Mary had been named for her much loved mother. They named their first child for Sidney's admirable sister, Margaret Pollock Sherwood.

But namesakes often suffer from their names. Mary Sherwood had been called "little Mary" to avoid confusion with other Marys in the family. She hated it. To spare their baby being called "little Margaret," her mother and father called her Gretchen, the German form of "little Margaret." A middle name, Merriam, was added in honor of a brilliant young scholar at Johns Hopkins, Lucius Merriam, who was very fond of baby Gretchen.

Aunt Margaret Pollock Sherwood, for better or worse, was

to have a great influence on her little namesake. By the time
Gretchen was born in 1892, Aunt Margaret had graduated
from Vassar with Phi Beta Kappa honors, had done graduate
work in Switzerland and at Oxford University. She had
earned a Ph.D. degree from Yale and was now teaching English at Wellesley College. She had had articles published in
the best literary magazines in America. Could the new baby
equal a record like that?

Mary began at once to put Gretchen on the road to college, a road that she herself had never been allowed to take.
The first step was through a love of books, beginning with
Mother Goose verses and fairy tales. When the Sherwoods
were living in Baltimore, Mary told Woodrow Wilson what
she read to her children. Professor Wilson, a conscientious
father and a serious scholar, said that he read Milton's
Paradise Lost and Wordsworth's poetry to his five-year-old
daughter. Why waste time on "Hey, diddle, diddle, the cat
and the fiddle"? Mary respected his opinion, but she could
always see the funny side, even of a learned professor. She
continued on her own way.

Gretchen soon was telling fairy tales of her own about
kings and princesses and palaces. At seven, she started
school at Baltimore's excellent Bryn Mawr Preparatory
School, where her aunt, Dr. Mary Sherwood, was the physician in charge of the students' health. Gretchen easily
learned to read and write. There were classes in storytelling
and in French songs and games. There were swimming
lessons as well, which pleased Mary.

The Bryn Mawr School assumed that almost all of its students would go to college, but somehow Gretchen understood very early that college was expensive and that fathers
could not always pay. One day she came home from school
saying that she could get a scholarship for college if she al-

ways learned her lessons but that she thought she would stay at home and give the money to her father. Perhaps it was an echo of her mother's often told story about giving up college; no one thought then that college expenses would be a serious problem for Sidney Sherwood's children.

Gretchen's early years in Baltimore were happy in the house at Roland Park, filled with her mother's chatter and laughter and her father's quiet love. (Their children called them ma*ma* and pa*pa* in the old-fashioned, formal way.) The house seemed beautiful because of its mahogany antiques, bookcases, and the carpets and tapestries brought back from Persia by the missionary Aunt Belle and her husband. The coming of three little sisters, Helen, Jean, and Penelope, made the household lively, but with a cook and a nursemaid, and with Sidney's help, Mary kept an orderly schedule. Everyone was up at half past six in the morning, and all except the youngest started the day with cold baths. After breakfast, Sidney took Gretchen and Helen to school by trolley before going on to his own work at the university. At night he helped put the children to bed, always with a romp or a story. Gretchen knew that he was often in his study late at night, absorbed in his reading and writing. It was probably Gretchen who remembered best how one night at dinner when they were all talking and laughing, Sidney said to his children, "You have the dearest little mother in the world. I want you to take care of her." At the time, it may have seemed a strange thing to say. Children did not take care of mothers; mothers took care of children. But Sidney's words had their effect.

Young as they were when Sidney died, Gretchen and Helen seemed to understand their mother's grief. They did try to take care of her, and little Jean and Penelope learned from Gretchen and Helen how to help.

Mary Sherwood needed all the help she could get. Sidney had left her an income of only twelve hundred dollars a year, including whatever pension or insurance he may have had. At first Mary seriously thought of taking her young family to live in Switzerland for a few years, perhaps at Lausanne, a beautiful resort city with good schools that were attended by many English-speaking students. Sidney had often talked about the benefits of European culture, and life abroad was cheap. Mary was strongly tempted. But Dr. Mary and Matt said that it would cost more than she expected; she would soon be cabling home to get baby Sidney out of pawn. Mary gave up the plan but never ceased to regret it. Gretchen may have heard some of the discussions and sympathized with her mother. Later she began to dream of someday living abroad herself.

Eventually Mary decided to sell the house at Roland Park, save that money for the children's education, and move back to Cornwall. She installed a coal furnace in the old house; the antique furniture and Persian carpets from Baltimore added a touch of elegance. Mary took care of the children and hired a Cornwall woman, Maggie, who had once helped Mary's own mother, to take charge of the cooking and housekeeping. Wages for domestic service were two or three dollars a week, which Mary would have to spend. Baby Sidney was frail and needed a great deal of attention. Each one of the children needed attention. She would not fail any one of them in any way.

In the fall of the first year at Cornwall, Gretchen and Helen went to the public school where as a child Mary had longed to go herself. Now she saw the school's shortcomings and was determined to make up for them. She wrote to the Bryn Mawr School for a schedule of their classes and found a high school graduate to tutor Gretchen and Helen and Jean in all the subjects that they would not have at Cornwall. Bryn Mawr was strong in the literature and foreign languages that would be required for college entrance exams. Mary read aloud before bedtime every night, sitting with the youngest child in her lap and the others gathered around her on the long back porch in the summer or around the fire by the bookshelves in the winter. She still read fairy tales but also read Charles Dickens's best-loved novels and Sir Walter Scott's stories about the Middle Ages and the Crusades; Woodrow Wilson would have approved. Gretchen's imagination was stirred. When her mother read aloud, time and place faded away and the characters of fiction became more real than her own family. The young tutor found that Gretchen took to French like a duck to water. She was quick and eager to learn and, like her father, never happier than at school.

As winter set in, Mary could say that her children were leading a good life. They had each other and schoolmates to play with. They had their favorite books to read and reread. There was a horse in the new barn, a collie dog, a kitten, and turtles, all of which the young Sherwoods fed and tended. There was ice skating on the pond and coasting down the hill behind the house on Mary's old sled. Uncle Matt and his wife had built a house where the old barn had stood and they often came up from New York for weekends and holidays. The children never felt lonely or bored.

For the first Christmas at Cornwall, Uncle Matt and his wife, Aunt Sallie, Aunt Margaret, and Dr. Mary all arrived on Christmas Eve to spend the night at 51 Angola Road. When the children had gone to bed, the grown-ups filled the stockings by the big hall fireplace and trimmed a tall tree. Before daylight the little girls were sliding down the banisters in their bathrobes and slippers, while Mary stoked the furnace and lit the fire in the hall. Matt and the aunties, too, appeared in their bathrobes for breakfast and the opening of presents, but soon afterward Matt went off. The girls, already in caps and coats, were waiting impatiently for him to come back and take them coasting when they heard sleigh bells and saw a Shetland pony coming along Angola Road, pulling a basket cart with red wheels, driven by Santa Claus. He drove up to the porch and called out, "Children, this pony is yours!" He had to take off his cap, wig, and beard before they knew it was Uncle Matt. With hugs and kisses for him and for the pony, they scrambled into the cart and had their first ride. The pony, named Gypsy, was to be their prized possession and friend for the next thirty years.

Another prized possession was also Uncle Matt's idea and gift. When he tore down the old barn, he was inspired to build a log cabin playhouse for the young Sherwoods at the far end of the garden so that they need not miss playing in the barn. A lumberman brought loads of chestnut logs and big stones for a foundation. During two summers, whenever Uncle Matt could spare time from his medical practice in New York City, he came up to work on the cabin, and the children helped. They peeled the bark from the logs and mixed mortar. They helped Uncle Matt measure and saw logs. They handed him nails and tools. The crowning glory of the cabin was the big stone chimney with a broad fireplace and old-fashioned bake oven. The stones above the mantel were the 130 specimens that Mary and her Agassiz Society friends had collected years before.

The second year, soon after Christmas, Gretchen had a setback. The winter was a cold one. Rain and freezing followed a heavy snowstorm, making a hard crust on the hillside behind the house. One morning before going to school,

The log cabin playhouse Uncle Matt built

Gretchen and Helen went out to coast on the old sled. Gretchen thought it would be fun to slide down the hill "belly-whoppers" and backward, without steering. Suddenly Helen ran into the house shouting, "Gretchen has broken her leg!" Maggie, the maid, ran with Mary to the foot of the hill where Gretchen was lying. She had bumped into an old stone wall and a heavy stone had fallen on her ankle. Helen had rolled it off, but both bones of Gretchen's leg were broken. She was in agonizing pain. Mary carried her up the long hill with Maggie supporting the broken leg. Since there was no telephone, Mary sent Helen running to the drugstore in Cornwall to call Dr. Harrison, a local doctor.

Inexcusably, Dr. Harrison made no effort to set the bones but simply put on a plaster cast. Mary saw that Gretchen's foot was twisted out of line. She asked Dr. Matt to come up from New York and give his opinion. Matt came at once, but Dr. Harrison refused to talk to him, and because of medical rules of etiquette, Matt could not remove the cast without Dr. Harrison's permission. Four weeks later, when Dr. Harrison himself removed the cast, Mary was shocked at what she saw. Gretchen's leg was badly out of line at the ankle. Matt then advised her to dismiss Dr. Harrison at once and tell him to send his bill. He never responded, nor did he send a bill. It may have been a silent acknowledgment that he had made a blunder.

Uncle Matt arranged for Mary to take Gretchen to a famous surgeon in New York, Dr. Charles McBurney, whose name is still known for his discoveries in diagnosing appendicitis. Dr. Mary came from Baltimore and Aunt Margaret from Wellesley to be with Mary through the ordeal. An X ray showed that a large amount of callus had formed but that the break had not yet healed. Dr. McBurney could repair the damage. In a forty-minute operation he broke up the callus, forced the leg and foot into correct position, and put on a new cast. When he came out of the operating room he told Mary, "Your little girl will have a strong leg, if not a perfectly straight one. She would never have walked on it if it had been left as I found it."

For thirteen weeks Gretchen did not walk, and she missed school. But the time was not lost. She kept up with schoolwork at home, and read, and wrote. In March 1903, she wrote a long poem for Dr. McBurney, beginning,

> One morning in the winter,
> Before we went to school,
> We thought we'd ride down on the crust
> 'Twas some time after Yule.
>
> I got my sleigh quite ready
> And down the hill I spun,

I bumped into the old stone wall
And oh! but it was fun!

Gretchen's poem ended,

I love Dr. McBurney
For making my leg straight
Or I would have been lame for life,
It would be a horrid fate!

During her months in a cast, Gretchen was also the chief writer for a monthly family journal, *The Elfin Magazine*, which may have been modeled on the magazine produced by Meg, Jo, Beth, and Amy in *Little Women*. The four Sherwood girls contributed stories, poems, news items, jokes, and riddles to their own magazine, the pages being written and illustrated by hand. Gretchen began to dream of being a poet, a dream that haunted her for years.

By June the cast was off, and she was limping only a little. Mary decided to leave baby Sidney at home with Maggie, under Aunt Sallie's supervision, and to take the little girls to visit Aunt Margaret at Wellesley College. It was an occasion that demanded the children's best clothes, and their Baltimore clothes were either worn out or outgrown. Mary was an expert with her mother's old sewing machine, but she had no time or money for the tucks and frills that were in fashion, and she had never really liked sewing, except for doll clothes. The little girls' dresses would be plain, but Mary bought four wide taffeta hair ribbons—blue, red, yellow, and pink—that perched on the children's heads like big butterflies, in the latest style. The hair ribbons would have to make up for things missing.

A great event of the week's visit at Wellesley was a performance of *Robin Hood* by students in the college's outdoor theater. The Sherwood children knew the story well, through Howard Pyle's *The Merry Adventures of Robin Hood* with its wonderful pictures, and they thought the story was especially for them because it took place in Sherwood Forest.

Another thrill at Wellesley was meeting Professor Katharine Lee Bates, head of the English department. She was already widely known and loved as the author of "America the Beautiful," which would later rival "The Star Spangled Banner" and "America" as the nation's favorite patriotic song. Miss Bates was a big woman with a deep, rich voice, and was a fascinating storyteller. One hot day she came for tea on Professor Margaret Sherwood's lawn and took all four of the young Sherwoods in her capacious lap, saying that she wished she had a dozen children. "America the Beautiful" seemed to have been written for the Sherwoods. To them, "Purple mountain majesties above the fruited plain" meant their mountains—Storm King, Deer Hill, and Black Rock— seen over the tops of their own apple trees. The children had sent copies of *The Elfin Magazine* to Miss Bates; she paid a dollar for her subscription and put her copies on file in the Wellesley Library. It was thrilling to have their work in a real library. It spurred Gretchen on with her writing.

One day after they returned home from Wellesley, they were lying on the grass listening to a story, when a carriage driven by a liveried coachman came into the driveway. Mrs. Charles Leigh Taylor had come to call with her ten-year-old daughter, Dorothy, who was just Gretchen's age. Mrs. Taylor's grandfather had founded Cornell University; she was rich in her own right and had married a rich man in the hotel business. The family were spending the summer on one of the big estates near the river and had seen the Sherwood girls in their pony cart driving through the village. Dorothy had no one to play with except a tutor who was giving her lessons. Mrs. Taylor invited Gretchen and Helen to play and have lessons with Dorothy. It was the beginning of a wonderful summer and even included a ride for Gretchen and Helen in Mr. Taylor's limousine, the first automobile in Cornwall.

There was only one point of disagreement between the two mothers. One day Mrs. Taylor came to 51 Angola Road with a bundle of Dorothy's outgrown but still beautiful hand-embroidered dresses. She offered them graciously and tactfully as a way for Mary to "save stitches." But Mary was annoyed. Sidney's children were provided for by what their own father's money could buy. Furthermore, Mary could not have some of her children dressed like heiresses and some left looking plainer than ever, by contrast. And what of the days when Gretchen and Helen went to the Taylors' house? They would feel awkward playing with Dorothy while wearing her clothes. Besides, they were happy with the dresses that Mary made for them and even happier splashing about in Idlewild brook, stark naked. To play in the water "bare naked," as they called it, was a way to get close to nature, and they loved it. Mary began to take them up into the hills to lovely and remote Sutherland's Pond, where her father had long ago taken his own children to swim. There they could strip off their clothes, plunge in, and swim like fish.

A friend had given the Sherwoods a second pony, and the Sherwood girls would ride off to the field below the house with homemade helmets, shields, and swords to play at fighting duels or being knights on crusades, like the knights in Sir Walter Scott's novels. From that summer onward, knights and heroes on horseback were a lifelong passion for Gretchen.

So she grew up, looking like what she was, a country girl. But Mary did not want her children to feel like country bumpkins. She organized a dancing class for the young Sherwoods and several of their friends at a nearby private school. They should feel at home on a dance floor; there would be proms when they went to college.

That time came early for Gretchen. She had just passed her sixteenth birthday when she entered Vassar College. Mary had decided on Vassar because it was nearby. The round-trip fare by train and river ferry was only ninety-eight cents, and Gretchen would be able to come home often. As for expenses, Gretchen's share of Mary's college savings fund would not be much, but Vassar was Aunt Margaret's college and Aunt Mary's; they could be counted on to write letters of recommendation and to give generous presents from time to time.

The greatest help of all was Gretchen herself. She won a scholarship, and her studies gave her no trouble, although she was the youngest in her class. She had mastered the art of concentration, which made learning easy and gave her an extraordinary sense of power and pleasure. It was the sort of pleasure her father had enjoyed when lost in his work. Gretchen, like her father, could be absorbed in, lost in, and in love with her work—as long as she liked the subject. English literature and foreign languages were her favorites.

Vassar was known, not quite fairly, as a rich girl's college. There were always rich students, but they were not conspicuous on most days. Everyone wore plain white middy blouses and ankle-length skirts to classes and went bareheaded on campus, their long hair pinned back into a knot or piled on top of the head like a cushion. Gretchen found kindred spirits at Vassar, made her own friends, and by Thanksgiving of her freshman year had invited one of them to come home to 51 Angola Road.

Gretchen as a college student

This was Prue Ellis, who came from Charles City, Iowa, and wrote home for permission to spend Thanksgiving with the Sherwoods. "Margaret Sherwood, a Freshman, has invited me to come home with her. She lives at Cornwall just down the river. They live on a farm right at the base of a mountain. They have four young children in the family and an aunt and uncle are going to be there. I met her mother and the children once this fall. Her mother was dear. But they are the most naive family you ever saw. [Gretchen's] mother does all the work for the family—washing and all. I could help get the meals and I should just love to do that—help about Thanksgiving dinner around in the kitchen. . . . The fare round trip, including ferry, is only 98 cents, so I think I can stand it financially. . . ."

During Thanksgiving weekend, Prue wrote again, and her letter gives the best picture we are likely to get of life at 51 Angola Road during Gretchen's freshman year at Vassar:

Dearest Father and Mother

You must always keep this letter, for probably I shall never write you one from a more beautiful place, nor in any other could you ever hear of more beautiful people than I am going to tell you about. I am writing in a cosy log cabin, flooded with sunlight, a fire popping and crackling in a great fireplace made of rocks of all kinds. In one corner there is a curious old, old flax spinning wheel, an old desk and old green chairs. . . . I am writing at an old table by the broad front windows of the cabin looking out on piles of sunny, dusty blue mountains and down below them all cunning little stone walls running up and down hills, and an apple orchard beyond them. . . . Gretchen is the oldest—she is at college now, was 16 in August and then comes Helen—she is 15. She's the most interesting of the family almost. She skins animals and stuffs them and loves to be out of doors. She is very reserved with people, but when she talks in her low deep voice she says things worth hearing. I like her! She is coming up to Ice Carnival with me. Then Jean comes next. She is the sweetest one of the family, they say. . . . Jean is 12 and Penelope 10. . . . Jean is a little taller and slenderer and has softer hair and prettier eyes. Penelope is round and sturdy! They both wear their hair bobbed—and little blue gingham dresses. Penelope is bossy and vigorous. . . . Of course "Syn" [Sidney] is the youngest. . . . (They're all out here, one popping corn and the others playing still-pond [statues].)

But oh I haven't told you about Mrs. Sherwood. I can't. She is little and brown and dear and strong. Just think she and her children keep house out here in the country in the nicest, simplest way. The house is most beautifully furnished with old mahogany furniture, and oriental rugs and Persian window curtains. But they live very simply really—the children help their mother in the dearest way. They take care of the horses and chickens too and help wash dishes. And their mother does it all so fast and joyously and she lets things go just before she gets too tired and she puts just enough emphasis on the importance of things and oh how she laughs! . . . the children adore her and it would be impossible for them not to. And Mrs. Sherwood is so interesting herself—besides being such a perfectly lovely mother. She uses most expressive words and really knows everything too. . . . Thanksgiving afternoon Mrs. Sherwood's doctor brother from New York and his wife were here. They were funny and jolly and interesting. Dr. Beattie took us up the mountains through ravines and to splendid views. Friday we walked up Storm King. . . . Oh I never have had such a wonderful time! I love you too, so much.

Your daughter Prue

Prue's visit was only one of many other weekends when college friends came home with Gretchen. Mary joined in everything they did, hiking, climbing, picnicking, and always coming back to 51 Angola Road for a big dinner that she had gotten ready before starting out for the day. She believed in good food as much as in good education, and never skimped. There would be a roast or steaks, fresh vegetables from the garden, homemade bread, and a dessert; Mary specialized in strawberry shortcakes. Afterward came the circle around the fire, reading aloud, telling stories, or talking and joking. Once Gretchen brought home twelve girls, and Mary sent a hay wagon to meet their train and drive them up the hill. The twelve wanted to sleep on the balcony above the long porch that looked toward the mountains. A door led out from the big upstairs bedroom to the flat roof, and the Sherwoods often slept there themselves, under the stars. The Vassar girls did little sleeping. They were laughing and singing most of the night.

Gretchen enjoyed life on campus, too. Lying to the east of the Hudson river town of Poughkeepsie, Vassar's broad lawns dropped to a lake where ice skating went on all winter. Beyond the lake, Sunset Hill and the higher Sunrise Hill were used for sledding and skiing. Gretchen became a champion skier. The college buildings impressed her, especially the handsome library, its square tower rising above the trees high enough to be seen from across the campus. At the end of the library's great hall a stained-glass window showed the figure of the seventeenth-century Italian lady Elena Lucrezia Cornaro, the first woman ever to be granted the doctoral degree. She had had a command of literature, rhetoric, logic, theology, music, and eight different languages. There she stood in glory, surrounded by learned professors after passing her examinations so long ago in Padua. It was an inspiration to look at her. Eight languages!

The Vassar faculty were real scholars, most of them members of Phi Beta Kappa and with doctoral degrees. Their message seemed to be "You can do it, too." Above all, there was Professor Jean Charlemagne Bracq, the head of the French department, a popular teacher, a notable scholar, a lover of France and all things French. Gretchen's pleasure in French took a leap forward. How far could she go with her French? Far indeed, as it turned out.

But most of all, she wanted to be a poet. She kept a journal, to which she confided her private thoughts and feelings that might be turned into poems later on. "It's a funny thing about poetry," she wrote in her journal, "but the parts that you work on the hardest are the worst." The search for the right word could be agonizing, and even if you found it, there was no guarantee that your poems would be printed. Most of Gretchen's never got into print.

Besides her intense desire to be a poet, other thoughts and dreams often overwhelmed her; she longed for love and marriage, because they must be the most intense of all poetic experiences. She wrote, "I must know the fullness of life to know poetry. I want to *know* a man—to conceive and bear fruit—For I can know *Life* only when I have produced it. . . . Yes, I must *love*, with soul and body, before I can be a true poet. . . . When I think of union with the man of my love, I see two tongues of flame coming together and shooting forth among the stars—a bright, passionate glory in the universe, illuminating space and all creation by the gleaming brightness of it. . . ."

The names of young men began to appear in the pages of Gretchen's journal: Jack, Hans, Harry, Walter, and others. Hans was at Haverford and sent her a college paper with poems written by his brother. "I wonder if I shall ever love him," Gretchen confided to her notebook. "Sometimes I think I shall, maybe, and then my heart warms up at the thought of being a wife and *creating* something really worthwhile. For to bring into the world and bring up lovely children is the highest and noblest kind of poetry and is the only real life. . . ." But poetry demanded total concentration, and so did the role of wife and mother. How could anyone do both?

On her last summer vacation, before her senior year, Gretchen had a narrow escape from death. Uncle Matt had rented a dune on the beach at Sagaponack, Long Island,

Helen, Sidney, and Gretchen at Sagaponack

and built a shack there with the help of the young Sherwoods. Mary had begun to take the family to the shack
every summer for a month of camping on the beach and
swimming. They all wore men's bathing suits, which were
light, close-fitting, and ended at the knees, unlike women's
bathing dresses. Sometimes the Sherwoods saw no one but
themselves all day long, and at night they could swim without suits. Gretchen had two college friends, Marjorie and
Mildred Wilson, granddaughters of the famous astronomer
Simon Newcomb, who spent their summers not far away at
East Hampton. It was a fashionable resort with strict rules,
and girls had to wear swimming dresses with full skirts.
The Wilson girls liked to come to Sagaponack and to borrow the Sherwoods' suits for a swim with a glorious sense
of freedom.

They happened to come to visit just after a wild three-day
storm. There were powerful "run outs" along the shore

where the water surged in and out again with great force. No lifeguard patrolled the beach at Sagaponack, but Uncle Matt had anchored a big rope fifty feet out from shore, and the Sherwoods had been told what to do if they were ever caught in a run out. When the Wilsons came, Gretchen put on one of their bulky bathing dresses and loaned her swimming suit. Then all of the young people ran to the water and plunged in, diving through the surf. Suddenly, Gretchen found herself caught in a powerful run out, being swept out into the deep water far from shore. Penelope called her mother, and Helen and Marjorie Wilson were about to dash in after Gretchen. With her strength almost gone, Gretchen managed to swim to the edge of the run out, as she had been told to do if she should ever be caught. Miraculously, she reached a sandbar, and a strong young neighbor came out with the rope around his waist to pull her to shore.

Afterward, Gretchen wrote about this terrible adventure in almost mystical terms: "I nearly drowned in the grip of the sea last summer—but I loved it; the feeling of being in the power of a mighty force and of not being afraid. Strength in submission, strength in waiting until the shoreward wave came to bear me to shore; that is power; that is mighty joy!"

But a mighty force seldom carried Gretchen along. She was often tormented by doubts that interfered with her work by breaking her concentration. As a poet, she was a failure. And if not a poet, what should she be after college? A political economist like her father? A doctor like Aunt Mary, giving real service in a practical way? Should she be a writer and teacher like Aunt Margaret? That seemed the best path to follow.

In February 1912, Gretchen was working hard toward her June graduation. Then came a blow. "Honors have been announced, and thirty-four in the class have them. But I haven't even Honorable Mention. I didn't know how much I wanted Honors until I didn't get them. I haven't really cried, but the disappointment is oh, so bitter! It is worse to have a mind and feel that you haven't used it, than not to have a mind at all. Oh, damn it! Everyone said I would get them, and that made me sanguine. . . . The worst of all this is that I have not borne out traditions of my fathers. To think that I can never have a Phi Beta Kappa key—the one that my [Sherwood] grandfather had!" Not only Gretchen's Sherwood grandfather had been a member of Phi Beta Kappa, at Union College in Schenectady; so had both Aunt Mary and Aunt Margaret at Vassar. Gretchen was heartsick. "Mamma would have been so happy if I had done well. Miss Wylie [the head of the English department] says that she expects me to get Honors, but that it doesn't matter at all, because I have *found myself,* which is the only important thing . . . but it doesn't take away the gnawing at my heart. Maybe, though, it's a good thing, because now I am going to study harder than ever. With God's help, I hope to win in the end, perhaps because of this rude jar to my self-conceit. . . . I am happy again, blissfully happy. . . . such a blessed letter from Mamma! It made me weep with joy in having such a mother, but with shame that I am not worthy of her and of Papa. . . ."

In March, another blow. Gretchen had applied for the Borden Fellowship, which provided for a year of study abroad, and her letter of application had been voted by the class to be one of the four best letters. High hopes were dashed; the fellowship went to another girl. But Gretchen had the satisfaction of knowing that the faculty and the class believed in her. "And because I didn't get it," she wrote, "I can do what I ought to and what I want to for Mamma"; that was, to spend the next year at home, proving that she, like Mary, could sacrifice selfish ambition for the sake of love.

Before the end of March came a total reversal of fortune. "March 24, 1912. The greatest, most wonderful joy of all—I can't believe that it is true—I have been elected to Phi Beta Kappa! An honor like that does not keep anyone else out, and it is so wonderful to think that you have justified all that has been spent on your education. I have *not* disgraced the family, and I can wear Grandpa's key. . . ." To top it all off, Hans invited her to a dance at Haverford.

Still, Gretchen's moods swung from exhilaration to deep gloom. April was a bad month. Only three months before graduation, and with her Phi Beta Kappa key in hand, she was writing:

I'm getting very envious and humble—in short, entirely dissatisfied with myself. I am, above all, common, unrefined—I don't see why I should be, but I am—and blunt and tactless and fickle. I have no personality . . . and I try to make an impression. . . . People in general like me, and other people are amused at me at first—but the very nicest people, the people I love and admire most, always like Helen much better than me. They feel the fineness of her nature. People think I'm kind of sweet and namby pamby like the old-fashioned heroine; Agnes in *David Copperfield,* for instance— and the girls say I'll be an old man's darling. But marriage wouldn't be marriage without the passion and fire of *youth* and the growing old together. . . . I'm so afraid that if I go home next year, I'll fall in love and not do any more studying. . . . And at home I always get thinking about Hans, while up here [at Vassar] he sort of fades away. I really am a fool.

By the end of May, Gretchen had another change of mind about what her work should be—not poetry, but folk tales and legends written so that old and young could enjoy them as she had enjoyed the great stories of the past read and reread by her own mother. "I am growing glad of my childlikeness," she wrote, "because I hope I may be able to help people just through simplicity and truth and faith. I think it will help me to live and understand the old stories of primitive peoples, and to bring them into the hearts and minds of my own contemporaries in a simple childlike way, in beautiful, common speech. I grow surer every day that I have found myself, my vocation at last; to bring up children in love and wonder for Nature and for the truly noble qualities in men. And this through the literature written when people still wondered at the world around them."

Without knowing it, she had put into words what would be the most important work of her life. But it was far from a final decision. Old doubts returned: "I don't think I have ever been in such distress of mind. Is it Senior year, with its uncertainty? Or is it because I am just waking up to the possibilities of life and my unfitness for them? O Papa how I wish you would talk to me now and inspire me with the right spirit. I believe I am the most ambitious and envious person that ever lived. And I cannot see my way out of this maze without your help. . . . How can I—oh, how can I gain strength and fortitude? I must find it in myself—but where? . . . I have returned to my childish pursuits and aspirations, after years of wandering—for now I am in love with poetry again and more ardently and truly than in my most zealous childhood days. . . ."

Gretchen's graduation picture shows her head poised gracefully on a slender neck that gives her a look of vulnerability. A band holds her dark hair back from a high forehead. Her face gazes dreamily into the distance.

But before Gretchen could turn dreams into reality, she had to go home. She went partly to help her mother, who had done so much for her, and partly to learn housekeeping, so that if she married, she herself could do the necessary work easily and quickly. It was a joy to have privacy again after four years of dormitory living. Gretchen moved her bed to the log cabin and reveled in having all her best-loved things around her. In October she continued her journal: "Here in the cabin—before the fireplace, where my little copper tea kettle is hanging—at my right the four-posted bed and mahogany bureau; at the left the spinning wheel, my bookcase with my dearest books—and a woodpile behind the door; back of me, out of the window, the mountains, gray and misty behind the nearer trees just turning red or yellow; out of the window toward the house—Jean's flower garden bright with marigold and cosmos gaily nodding. And yet—I am so unsettled. . . ."

Gretchen's trouble was that "all the people with the best minds" were going into social work, and the need was great. Was it right for her to devote herself to literature and the past? Wasn't it a waste of time and energy when the present was crying out for attention? Her own mother was no longer spending all of her energy on her home and family, now that her children were growing up; she no longer seemed the same person whom Gretchen had known.

Mary was as loving as ever and as ready to promote her children's happiness and success, but one by one they were leaving the nest. Helen was at Vassar, Jean and Penelope were in Cornwall High School. Only Sidney was still a child. Mary's energy needed new outlets, and she knew in what direction she should go. She would follow the lead of other New York State women who had been pioneers for causes important to women. They were a noble band of idealists.

Lucretia Mott, a Quaker, had studied and taught at a Friends' school near Poughkeepsie. She had lectured on temperance, on peace, and on women's rights. A younger reformer, Elizabeth Cady Stanton, had joined Mrs. Mott in her work, and together, in 1848, they had organized the first women's rights convention in the United States. That meeting, at Seneca Falls in upstate New York, was still talked about, with admiration by some, with alarm and disgust by others. Mrs. Stanton had been educated at an academy, now the Emma Willard School at Troy, New York, which taught subjects not usually offered to girls; she was a brilliant orator.

These two powerful women were followed by Susan B. Anthony, who became a patient and a close friend of Dr. Mary Sherwood in Baltimore. Miss Anthony was the daughter of a Quaker abolitionist. As a girl she had taught in rural New York schools but soon began to agitate for causes related to equal rights for women, especially women's suffrage, the right to vote, a cause deeply interesting to Dr. Mary. Austere in face and dress, Miss Anthony brought the whole force of her great intelligence and strong personality to focus on this cause with the driving force of an arrow, but it would be a long struggle.

The right to vote appealed strongly to Gretchen's mother for personal reasons. One election day, she had looked out her window and had seen a neighbor, an illiterate man, on his way to the polls to cast his vote by "making his mark," since he could not write his name. Saloons had been abolished in Cornwall by local legislation, but a proposal to legalize them was being voted on this election day. Mary was sure how her neighbor, a drinker, would vote. It infuriated her that she, an educated woman, could not take a part in voting against the evil that had helped to destroy her brother Frank. When Susan B. Anthony, at the age of eighty, organized the first suffrage parade in New York City, Mary Sherwood was one of the two thousand marchers. They paraded from Washington Square up Fifth Avenue to Fifty-ninth

Street, wearing white straw hats shaped like beehives—unbecoming, in Mary's opinion, but at least uniform. At the head of the parade in an automobile rode Miss Anthony with Dr. Mary Sherwood at her side in her academic cap and gown. Afterward, Gretchen's mother found ten women in Cornwall who were willing to work for women's suffrage, and on August 18, 1910, she called to order the first meeting of the Cornwall Woman's Suffrage Club on her back porch.

When Gretchen returned home from Vassar after graduation, she found Mary busy with the suffrage club. Mary had also organized a PTA at the Cornwall public school and had organized or joined half a dozen other groups, including the Village Improvement Society. She found teachers for groups of her friends who wanted private lessons in German and Spanish. She was the chairman of the Campfire Girls. Under her leadership the members of the Improvement Society, in short skirts and rubber boots, were cleaning out Idlewild Brook. The Boy Scouts were meeting once a week in the cabin.

None of it appealed to Gretchen. Her mother found time to teach her cooking and housekeeping and sewing, but there was no privacy for studying, dreaming, and writing when even the cabin was invaded by Boy Scouts.

Then Aunt Margaret came to visit and urged Gretchen to find a job teaching in some school. If she really wanted to help her mother, she should earn some money. Why couldn't she write while teaching, as Aunt Margaret did? Until now, Gretchen had secretly found Aunt Margaret rather formidable, but she seemed to have mellowed, and Gretchen was not ungrateful for the hundred dollars that her aunt had sent, besides Christmas and birthday presents, during each of her college years. Out of respect and gratitude to Aunt Margaret, Gretchen took her advice. She found a teaching job for the following year, 1914, at Drew Seminary for Girls in Carmel, New York.

The year was a disaster. Carmel was only twenty miles east of Cornwall, but in spirit the school seemed a thousand miles from home. Gretchen quickly discovered that she was not a good teacher, and she disliked the work. By December 1914, she was writing in her journal: "Themes! Themes! Themes! I don't dare look at the pile in my drawer—I have too much work to do it efficiently, so I hate to do it." Adding to her unhappiness, there was dissension among the teachers. A girl was caught cheating and talked her way out of a punishment. Many of the boarding school students lacked something essential; they seemed never to have had a home. Gretchen wrote to her mother: "These homeless girls seem not to know what a real home life is. I think one day spent with us at Cornwall would open their eyes to the true meaning of life and love."

Worst of all, even as she wrote these words, she was possessed by a demon that ruined her own thoughts of home. She was feeling intensely jealous of Helen, who was, in fact, neither as pretty nor as gifted as herself. She confided to her journal: "The galling thorn in my flesh is Helen. Ever since I can remember I have been jealous of her. I have always had to be doubly sweet when she was bad—Mamma demanded it of me; whatever I have started she has finished with glory and honor. I break the ice for her success. . . . It has always galled me like chains of slavery—and yet I love and admire Helen more than I do anyone else. I could accomplish more if I were not so envious of her. I think this jealousy will be the ruin of my power. . . . Mamma does think that I shall do a great work well and nobly, but she thinks of Helen in a special light—I am her confidante, Helen is her darling. Of course, Mamma has never shown, or, I believe, thought this; but I know that it is so." In May 1915 she took it all back: "I absolutely disavow the beginning of this entry. In the 'baptism of fire' which I have undergone, Mamma has stood by me as no one else could have. . . . The midnight oil has been burning for me this week, with no better result than a few hundred themes handed back to the owners— besmeared and o'ertripped by crimson ink—my heart's blood I guess by the dizzy condition of my head. . . . I'd like to attend some of my own classes to see how it feels to be sat on as heavily and bumpily as I sat on my gasping pupils to-day."

As a teacher she was in a run out. Should she struggle on? she asked herself, or "Will time and tide decide it for me? I feel powerless; I must trust to the shoreward wave. I may be set high and safe on the shore and I may just as probably be engulfed in the destroying waters. . . . I said the struggle was fun—maybe it is when you have come safely out of it! . . ."

At the end of the school year, Gretchen left Drew Seminary with relief; it is not known whether the school regretted her going.

Her inner conflicts were nothing compared with the great conflict that broke out in August 1914, as the First World War began in Europe. Woodrow Wilson was president in the White House and promised to keep the United States out of the war. But even if he succeeded, France and Germany were enemies, and it was hard for Gretchen to feel like the enemy of either country. Like most Americans, the Sherwoods had many friends of German background; she herself spoke German fluently and had been a member of the German Club at Vassar. They sang *"Stille Nacht"* and *"O Tannenbaum"* for the whole college every Christmas. And Gretchen had fallen in love with the music of Richard

Wagner. The "Fire Music" from *Die Walküre* sent her into ecstasies. She saw herself as Brünnhilde, daughter of the gods, asleep within a magic circle of fire. She saw Siegfried, the unknown and perfect hero, riding through the flames to awaken her.

But France was even dearer to her heart than Germany. Professor Jean Charlemagne Bracq had lit a fire of enthusiasm in his students for what he called "the France that is the noblest nation in Europe . . . the France that has never thought an idea truly great unless it radiated as an inspiration to the world." The senior class had dedicated its yearbook to Professor Bracq because he had "given to the college the devoted service of many years and to the cause of international understanding his enthusiastic support." But in 1914, international understanding was at best a dim hope. For Gretchen the outbreak of war was the climax of what she called "the most horrible year I have ever known; from the gloom of a fearful war; from the depths of gloom in my own heart, a gloom inspired by work I cannot do well, and worst of all by jealousy of Helen, most dearly beloved of all my sisters, by uncertainty of my ability. . . ."

Then, in spite of all conflicts, light seemed to dawn for Gretchen. After a visit to Vassar for consultation with her old teachers in the English department, she decided to go to New York and get a job as proofreader for some publisher— any publisher that would hire her. Proofreading would not be inspiring; like teaching English, it meant correcting the mistakes of other writers, and it was not well paid or steady work. But if she could manage to exist, combining jobs with study at Columbia University, there might be a great reward in the end—a Ph.D. degree. To have that, as her Aunt Margaret did, would prove her own ability. And she would be living for the first time in what undergraduate students called, and still call, "The Outside World . . . the Real World." Gretchen plunged into it.

The real world was a shock. She started but could not finish a short story based on her impressions of life in New York City: her first cigarette, her first glass of wine, of champagne, of beer, of staying up half the night exchanging wild tales with new friends. What would Mamma have said, if she had known!

At Columbia Gretchen impulsively took courses in economics, out of devotion to her father's memory; she took journalism out of respect for Aunt Margaret's advice. Yet in some moods she still longed to be a poet, living in poverty forever if need be, rather than let money rule her life. In the end she decided that the Romance languages—Latin, French, Italian, Spanish, and Portuguese—were her greatest strengths, the Old French of the Middle Ages being her favorite. But how could she earn a living in Romance languages? Sooner or later she would have to face that problem.

On April 6, 1917, while Gretchen was still working toward a Ph.D. at Columbia University, the United States declared war on Germany and its allies. Among the students there were heated debates about the issues of pacifism and militarism. A month later, Gretchen made her last long entry in her journal, describing the visit to New York City of the French general known as "Papa" Joffre. He was the hero of the early battles of the war, and he was mobbed by wildly enthusiastic crowds. Only ten feet away from Gretchen, he stood on a platform, a sea of people surging around him. Thousands of schoolchildren pressed around the platform to see him receive a gift from the city, a small copy of the Statue of Liberty in gold, on a silver pedestal. He was wearing a handsome light blue cloak and a scarlet and gold cap. As Gretchen saw it, "All that 'Papa' Joffre has to do is to salute and sometimes smile or kiss his finger tips or the cheeks of a little girl, or say 'Vive l'Amérique,' and he comes in for such a round of cheering and yelling that you would think the millennium was being ushered in." All day long there were ceremonies and parades, and the whole city went mad with excitement. Everyone was singing the new song "Over There." Many Columbia student recruits already wore the khaki uniform of the American Expeditionary Forces. "It is funny how theories melt away before the fierce rays of an inevitable calamity," Gretchen wrote. "I can no longer think in terms of pacifism and militarism. Our paths, as individuals, seem unmistakably plain all of a sudden. . . ."

At home, Mary Sherwood was heading a group of women who worked at the Red Cross headquarters in Cornwall twelve hours a day, six days a week, rolling bandages and making clothes for victims of the war in France. The Christmas of 1917 was a quiet one. Gretchen went home to Cornwall, but there were no presents. Money went to the Red Cross instead.

The last day Gretchen wrote in her journal was July 5, 1918: "The *Times* reads: Reported July 4—killed in action: Roland Jackson, Lieutenant. 228 E. Kiowa St., Colorado Springs, Colorado." Whatever the name Roland Jackson meant to Gretchen, all over the United States girls were reading the same kind of news, the deaths of young men they had known as boys who went "over there."

On November 11, 1918, the war ended. It was like the clearing of the sky after a long and terrible storm. And suddenly, Gretchen had the chance of a lifetime. The University of Grenoble in the southeastern part of France asked Vassar College to recommend a graduate who was qualified to teach English as a second language. Professor Jean Charlemagne Bracq had not forgotten his Phi Beta Kappa student who had done outstanding work in French and in English courses and who now had a Ph.D. in Romance languages from Columbia University. Professor Bracq recommended Margaret Merriam Sherwood to Vassar's president, Dr. Henry Noble Mac-Cracken, and as a result Gretchen sailed for France.

France was all and more than she had hoped. Grenoble was a big city with a fine university. For the first time, Gretchen saw houses, churches, and monasteries that were already old before the discovery of America. She seemed to have walked straight into the France of the Middle Ages. It was a dream come true. She spent her Christmas holidays skiing in the French Alps. She played cards and danced with peasants in an Alpine village that had been cut off from the rest of the world by an avalanche. She climbed among rocks and glaciers with her pupils and drank hot wine, or bowls of milk, in lonely shepherds' huts and little inns below the snow line. She became friends with old royalist Catholic families and wrote to President MacCracken: "I have grown to love most ardently the complex French character, so different from our own. . . . To arrange international matters we must *know* other nations and make allowances for differences of custom and character. . . ." Now, at last, she thought, she knew what she *really* wanted to do; she should study diplomacy and help to heal the wounds of the nations of the world, beginning somehow in France.

Unfortunately, in March 1920, Gretchen had to write again to President MacCracken:

> Will you pardon me for writing you very frankly about the ridiculous and embarrassing situation in which I find myself?
> My salary here at the University is, as perhaps you remember, very small indeed (this year it is 2200 francs [about $500]), for the year with a supplement of 60 francs a month for the first three months. This just pays for my board and

lodging in winter. In summer I am not paid, and last summer was obliged to spend two months with a French family, speaking English for my board. . . . You can easily understand that it has been impossible for me to save any money. I find myself, therefore, in the humiliating position of being unable to pay my passage home with the present terrifically high exchange rate. It is absolutely imperative for me to return . . . for, although Mamma says little about it, I know she is having a hard struggle to make both ends meet. . . . This is why, after much hesitation, I write to ask if it would be possible for me to borrow with interest $100.00 from Vassar College to pay my passage home. . . .

It had been almost twenty years since Dr. Mary and Uncle Matt had warned Gretchen's mother that life abroad cost more than she thought, and that if she went, she might have to pawn baby Sidney to get home. Gretchen had no baby to pawn, her only security, as she said, "being my good health and the certainty of obtaining a good position next year with my equipment, the Ph.D. degree in Romance Languages and nearly two years' continuous residence in France. . . . I am almost sure I could pay back the loan next year. . . ."

President MacCracken responded promptly, cabling a hundred and fifty dollars to Gretchen with the comment that the college owed her some help because they had recommended her to the University at Grenoble.

In thanking him, Gretchen wrote that it had long been a dream of hers to get into diplomatic work. Perhaps she could find some position at the American Embassy at Paris. Among her qualifications she listed an unusual one: "I am not, like many college women, simply an 'intellectual.' Mamma taught us practical things, and I can make an American middy blouse to please a little French girl as well as or better than I can teach her to pronounce 'th!' I can discuss the relative value of wood and coal as fuel with the old lady who lives next door; or make a delicious soup out of the remains of my rucksack's contents at a refuge 2500 m. high and only use a handful of wood to cook it. It is above all the simplicity of my early training which has brought me near to the hearts of the people I have known. . . ." She wrote of beginning Russian and brushing up on her German. Eight years after graduation from college, she was still thrashing about trying to free herself from the hook on which she was caught, the need to teach. Teaching was the only way that had yet appeared as a practical means to earn her living and help her mother.

It was humiliating to come home penniless, but she found Mary in high spirits. Women had won the right to vote. The Cornwall Woman's Suffrage Club met on Mary's back porch to disband, but they continued to interest themselves in state, national, and world affairs. Gretchen joined in none of these activities. She disliked meetings and organizations. Whatever the reason, when her mother registered as a Democrat, Gretchen registered as a Republican. She may also have had mental reservations about the news that her sister Jean, a 1918 Vassar graduate, had been recommended by President MacCracken to tutor Anna and Elliott Roosevelt at the big estate in Hyde Park. Their father was the vice-presidential nominee of the Democratic party.

Gretchen had no choice but to teach again, this time as assistant professor of French at Wells College in Aurora, New York. The following year she was teaching French at Smith College; perhaps the salary was bigger. But money was never Gretchen's first consideration, and by 1924 she was at Columbia once more, taking a step back, in both salary and rank, but happy to be in the stimulating atmosphere of the big city. She was now only a graduate lecturer on Old

French in the department of Romance languages, and she was paid on a fee basis, depending on the number of students in her classes. Since few students wanted to learn Old French, she could expect to earn no more than two or three hundred dollars. To add to her income she wrote encyclopedia articles for a publisher and even did research on a history of retailing for a New York department store. It was Grub Street at its worst. Gretchen's only pleasure came from work for President MacCracken. He understood her and became almost a second father to her. He, too, was an ardent scholar, spending all his free time in studying the minor poems of an obscure English poet, John Lydgate. He hired Gretchen on a month-to-month basis to do research for him. It was just the kind of thing she loved, and, as it turned out, their work together went on for years.

Then came the opening of the Pierpont Morgan Library at Madison Avenue and Thirty-sixth Street, a treasure house of illuminated medieval manuscripts and rare books, a gift to the public for the use of scholars. Gretchen had a brainstorm. Here was a way out of dreary teaching and hack writing. She wrote to Mr. C. C. Stillman, an old Cornwall friend of her mother and a man with wide connections among influential people. She spelled out the details of what she wanted: in short, a lifelong income, starting at five thousand dollars a year, to work full time in the Pierpont Morgan Library, or another library of the same kind, doing research and writing in peace and quiet. No more teaching.

Nothing came of her dream. Yet the best of all her dreams did come true. In the department of Romance languages at Columbia Gretchen met Harold Elmer Mantz, who had earned his own Ph.D. at Columbia. Since then, he had been teaching and writing scholarly articles about medieval manuscripts. He went to France as often as possible. He was the right age, four years older than Gretchen, but not quite as tall. He was not Siegfried. He wore glasses. In contrast with the style of the day, his hair was rather long and untidy. In the company of the Sherwood family, who never stopped talking, he was quiet and withdrawn. He was no knight on horseback. But for Gretchen he was much better. He was a kindred spirit, had a good sense of humor, and lived on East Thirty-sixth Street, a short walk from the Pierpont Morgan Library. His apartment was lined with rare books from floor to ceiling.

He and Gretchen decided to go into partnership as scholars. He had been married once before, and divorced, which may explain a detail in a letter that Gretchen wrote to Dr. MacCracken at the end of summer 1925: "I think I ought to announce to you a reorganization of our 'firm.' On August 10, I was married to my partner, Dr. Mantz. We did not have a wedding, and I asked Mamma not to send out regular announcements. . . . Professionally I shall keep my own name, but not socially. So I prefer to have it as I wrote you. Very cordially yours, Margaret Sherwood Mantz."

The question of her name was giving Gretchen other problems. Editors and publishers assumed that a manuscript from "Margaret Sherwood" was from Aunt Margaret Sherwood, *the* Margaret Sherwood, the successful writer who was still going from glory to glory and had now been given an honorary degree by New York University. It was irksome to Gretchen. She had lived for long enough under the shadow of Aunt Margaret. She decided to drop "Margaret" altogether and use only her middle name. From now on she would be "Merriam Sherwood." Her husband, too, used only his middle name, signing himself "Elmer Mantz," avoiding "Harold" for some reason of his own.

Almost at once the partnership and marriage bore fruit,

not the children for whom Gretchen had once longed, but books, publishable books by Merriam Sherwood.

The first was for children, eight to ten years old. It was called *The Merry Pilgrimage* and was translated and introduced by "Merriam Sherwood." The story came from an old French poem, *"Le Pélerinage de Charlemagne"* ("The Pilgrimage of Charlemagne"), telling "how Charlemagne went on a pilgrimage to see whether Hugo of Constantinople was a handsomer man than he." The story had been sung by minstrels for ordinary, simple people, and Merriam Sherwood gave a colorful picture of a holiday crowd at Saint-Denis, a shrine of France's patron saint. The crowd were gathered around a minstrel, "laughing until the tears rolled down their cheeks and holding their sides with mirth" to hear how the great emperor of France, Charlemagne, and his best knights once made fools of themselves; how returning from Jerusalem on horseback, carrying holy relics, they came to the magnificent palace of King Hugo, rich in gold and silver furniture, in priceless paintings, and in bronze figures of children blowing ivory trumpets. Charlemagne had never seen the like. "If the wind, blowing from the sea, smote the palace on the western side it would turn swiftly, like the wheel of a chariot revolving on the ground. And the horns of white ivory would blow and bugle and resound, like drums or thunder or a great swinging bell." Then Charlemagne and his knights boasted secretly among themselves about the stupendous deeds they could do to bring King Hugo and all his men to shame. But a spy heard them and told King Hugo what they had said. King Hugo demanded that they carry out their threats, on pain of death, and the Emperor Charlemagne feared for his life. But an angel worked miracles to help all the Frenchmen fulfill their boasts—on condition that they should never boast again.

The story was full of magic and laughter. The title appeared on highly recommended lists of books for children; Merriam Sherwood had succeeded in doing what she had hoped for long ago in college, "to love and understand the old stories of primitive peoples, and to bring them into the hearts and minds of my own contemporaries in a simple, childlike way, in beautiful, common speech." One of the first copies of *The Merry Pilgrimage* was inscribed "For Mamma with Gretchen's love, September 22, 1927."

In 1928 came another success, *The Road to Cathay* by Merriam Sherwood and Elmer Mantz. It was an account of early travels by five Europeans into the mysterious Orient. One of these adventurers was Marco Polo. Asia's vast deserts, its caravansaries, its fabulous palaces, and its long history of terrifying and bloody devastation by barbaric hordes, all were seen by the reader as the travelers had first reported them, and were illustrated with colored picture maps. *The Road to Cathay* was reviewed by important papers and journals and was recommended for readers of any age. *The Horn Book*, a journal devoted to books for young readers, said: "In *The Road to Cathay* two scholars and an artist . . . have combined to present a gorgeous book of the little known East of the Middle Ages." Each chapter title lured the reader along the journey: "The Golden Horde" . . . "Of the Great City of Cambaluc" [Cambaluc was the "Xanadu" of Kubla Khan, later Peking, and the Beijing of today] . . . "Cathayan Marvels." The travelers came home by way of Persia, a country that had fascinated Gretchen from her earliest days. Aunt Belle Sherwood Hawkes and her husband, James, had brought home from Persia not only the Persian rugs that lavishly carpeted the plain old farmhouse on Angola Road, but romance woven into the Sherwoods' everyday life as well. It was probably from the

Persian rugs as much as from *The Arabian Nights* that Gretchen got her childhood impressions of Oriental splendor; the work of Aunt Belle and her husband, James Hawkes, on a Persian Bible may have sparked her first interest in foreign-language translations. Whatever its roots may have been, the fruit was sweet. The two authors inscribed a copy of *The Road to Cathay* "To Mamma with love from Gretchen—To Mary with love from Elmer." It was soul-satisfying to have written "a gorgeous book," published by Macmillan, and to have written it together.

Nothing succeeds like success. In 1930 Bertha Gunterman, the distinguished children's book editor at Longmans, Green and Company, published *The Tale of the Warrior Lord*, Merriam Sherwood's retelling of the Spanish epic whose hero was the Cid. Here again was a knight on horseback, the greatest knight of Spain; *The Horn Book* carried a long article about the new book, saying that retellings of old fairy tales and legends were getting much attention in fresh versions that "are not really bringing forth the work of a single mind, but the cumulative dreams of all the ages." The story of *El Cid* had been written down by a poet monk in 1307. Now six hundred years later, Merriam Sherwood had brought it to life again. "Thus are great legends carried forward from age to age," said the reviewer.

Ceaseless efforts to write well, long years of research, and a happy marriage to a sympathetic husband all seemed to be carrying Merriam Sherwood forward on a wave of good fortune at last. Luckily, just at this time, publishers, critics, teachers, and parents saw children's books not only as stories about modern children, for modern children, but as part of the great sea of literature, old as the world, but fresh for each new swimmer who plunged into it. Few people knew who Merriam Sherwood was, or even whether Merriam was a man or a woman, but they knew that books by this writer treated readers with respect, spreading out marvels for their wonderment. Merriam Sherwood made twentieth-century boys and girls see knights on horseback riding out from their castles and hear the trumpets blowing from the towers.

Merriam Sherwood applied several times for scholarships to study abroad but was turned down again and again. Meanwhile, she and Elmer Mantz, as a team, were earning enough to breathe more easily. She continued to teach Old French to a few students at Columbia; he taught courses in mysticism at Columbia and at Cooper Union. In their free time they translated and wrote scholarly articles on obscure subjects, for which they were paid little or nothing. They lived simply. Then came a windfall. A professor in the history department at Columbia was doing some work on the Middle Ages in France; he recommended Merriam for a fellowship as his helper. Early in 1934 she wrote to President MacCracken with the joyful news: "I have been awarded a fellowship of $2,400 by the Council on Research in the Humanities. I am to work for a year or more, principally in Toulouse. . . . I expect to go early in June."

Toulouse! The gateway to the Pyrenees, gateway to summer climbing and picnicking, to winter skiing, to all-year-round festivals in little mountain villages, to religious pilgrimages, to legends. A scholar of the Middle Ages would at once think of Roncesvalles, at a high pass in those mysterious Pyrenees. There, according to legend, the French long ago had fought a fatal rear-guard action on their return from wars in Spain. They had been led by Charlemagne's nephew, Roland. Unforgettable, never to be forgotten, Roland had become the hero of the great French epic, *La Chanson de Roland (The Song of Roland)*. Outnumbered, the French had fought valiantly to the last man, and that last

man was Roland. Too proud to sound his ivory horn to sum-
mon Charlemagne's aid, he had fallen, facing the foe, and
had thereby won immortality even in defeat. Too late,
Charlemagne had returned, repulsed the enemy, and
avenged Roland's death with great slaughter, never to be
forgotten except perhaps by a new generation of young
Americans. They had heard of the World War fought in
France, the war to which young Americans of 1917 had gone
"over there"; they had heard of many thousands, like Roland
Jackson, who had fought in France with terrible loss of life.
Had they ever heard of Roland of France?

Merriam Sherwood began work on a translation of *The
Song of Roland*. Before she finished it, Elmer Mantz became
ill. He died of cancer in New York City on May 3, 1939, at
the age of fifty-one. But Merriam's new book was published
in 1938. Elmer must have seen it, the best of her work. The
stern music of France's great poem, chanted by minstrels for
hundreds of years, still thrilled French hearts and all lovers
of "Sweet France." Now *The Song of Roland* would thrill
English-speaking readers in Merriam Sherwood's words. She
had wanted to be a poet; she had wanted to become a diplomat, helping to promote international understanding. In a
strange way, she had achieved both goals. She had retold in
translation a great old story so that even children of another
language could respond to its beauty and tragedy. "High
were the peaks, and shadowy and tall; the valleys deep; and
swift, the streams. The clarions sounded in the van and in
the rear, all taking up and prolonging the voice of Roland's
horn. The Emperor rode in wrath; and the French, sor-
rowful and angry. Not one was there but wept and lamented,
praying God to protect Roland until they might all join him
on the field of battle. What blows they would deal by his
side! Of what avail their prayers? Prayers could not help

them now. They had waited too long and could not arrive in time. . . ."

There is a photograph of Mary Sherwood, taken on the lawn at Cornwall in 1941; she is an old woman, seventy-seven years old, reading a typed manuscript, "The Feel of France," by Merriam Sherwood. Mary looks earnest and intent, as if to see into its meaning and into the mind of the writer, Margaret Merriam Sherwood Mantz. Mary's daughter Gretchen had become another person. Spellbound, she had been carried on a great wave of time and fate into the past of "Sweet France."

After Elmer's death she bought a house in the medieval village of Céreste in the south of France, a house built of ancient stone; a parlor, a kitchen, two bedrooms, and a cellar. Across a path was a footbridge leading to an old coach house, where a big upper room became Gretchen's study and the stable below became a kitchen and dining room that opened onto a garden surrounded on two sides by the old town wall. To Gretchen it was a dream house. She planned to live at Céreste as much as possible. She hoped that her family would come to visit her, but she would seldom be coming home to Cornwall.

Mary could not foresee the end of Gretchen's story. There were to be fifteen years of government service as senior translator for the State Department in Washington, D.C., a translator not only of Old French but of many languages. During those years Gretchen was always looking forward to the time when she could retire, live permanently at Céreste, and give herself up to writing. Aunt Margaret had written in her last novel, *Pilgrim Feet*, "What was the escape of travel, of new horizons, in comparison with the great escape of utter surrender, the vanishing of self in creative activity?" Creative activity—that was the great wave to which her name-

*The village of Céreste, France. Gretchen's home, at center right,
consists of the two buildings facing onto an open yard with a tree
in the center, enclosed by the town walls.*

A view of Gretchen's house

sake, Margaret Merriam, wanted to surrender, in which to vanish and drown.

At long last, in 1960, Gretchen retired to Céreste. Without apology she turned away from the present to the past, writing to Vassar classmates: "Some old things, books and ideas and history, must be preserved as ballast or we shall all founder in space." She was writing a book on the Crusades when she died in 1961.

Six years later her family gave a bronze sculpture to Vassar College in memory of Margaret Merriam Sherwood. It was called *The Crusader*—the figure of a medieval warrior, mounted on a spirited horse and trampling a dragon. The statue of the Crusader is part of Penelope's story.

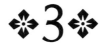

HELEN

I n naming their second child Helen, Mary and Sidney may have hoped that she would be beautiful like the legendary Helen of ancient Greece, but Helen Sherwood was not beautiful, and there was something "different" about her, especially when compared with Gretchen. They were born only fourteen months apart, and their parents treated them as a pair, Gretchen-and-Helen, but Gretchen was pretty and quick to learn. Helen was plain and slow. She had to go at her own pace.

It may have taken some time for her mother, Mary, to understand this, since she herself moved quickly and did things easily. For example, the family went to live at Roland Park when Helen was a baby. On moving day, as they arrived at the empty house, Fanny, the maid, dropped the bag in which she was carrying all of the baby's bottles, filled with pasteurized milk. Mary, unruffled, simply borrowed a tin cup from a carpenter who was working in the house, hailed a passing milkman, and boiled some fresh milk in time to feed Helen. By three o'clock, the moving van had come and gone, the furniture was in place, and Mary was calmly planning a dinner party to be served that night for seven adults. Dr. Mary Sherwood and her partner, Dr. Lilian Welsh, the guests of honor, were sailing for Europe the next day, and Mary could not, would not, let them go without entertaining them. Helen did not inherit these talents. Mary often became impatient with her and at the same time was protective of this "different" child.

Helen seemed to live in a world of her own. Animals, birds, flowers, trees, earth, air, water, and sky were almost as important to her as Papa and Mamma, Gretchen, and later on, Jean, Penelope, and the little brother, Sidney, Jr. The security of home was very important to Helen, especially the old farmhouse at Cornwall, where she spent every year of her childhood after her father's death; a large part of her security came from the life she lived outdoors there. Nature was an intense joy to her and also a comfort in time of trouble.

One troubled day when she was three years old, still living in Baltimore, Woodrow Wilson came to lunch, and Helen was allowed to sit at the table. When she misbehaved, her mother sent her to stand in the corner. Later, Mary remembered how Helen "stood quietly, with her face to the wall, whispering to herself a little story about 'Mr. Wind and Mr. Wind's horse.'" Perhaps Mary had read her Robert Louis Stevenson's poem, "Windy Nights":

> Whenever the moon and stars are set,
>   Whenever the wind is high,
> All night long in the dark and wet,
>   A man goes riding by. . . .

The real wind and real horses would always mean more to Helen than a poem about them, but "Mr. Wind and Mr. Wind's horse" gave her an escape route from punishment in the corner of the dining room. She learned many poems by heart. Once a week the children in the first grade at Bryn Mawr School learned poems to recite.

One poem, by her father, Helen loved and recited as long as she lived. Sidney's poem was about having the courage to get up and go on after falling; it was about having faith in the future, no matter how bleak the present might be:

> . . . that faith intense
> Which will not mutely rest in present ill;
> We nothing have that gives us true content,
> But struggle onward and with force ne'er spent
> Rise from our hundred falls to fight on still. . . .

Her father's poem was a legacy much needed by a child like Helen, who was fated to have a "hundred falls" of many kinds.

In a journal that she kept after college, she once jotted down what she called "Snapshots of my childhood."

Very few memories before eight years. Children in Roland Park. Papa on streetcar going to work and [taking] me to school, and making a cigar. Interest in birds. . . . Naturalist's love of all forms of life. Papa's sickness at Ballston. Fear in house. Aunt Margaret's and [Dr.] Mary's hushed voices. Dread.

News of Papa's death. Said Mamma must find new Papa. Could not accept. Indelible face in coffin and mourning and Mamma's white face all that fall. Guilt. Told Mamma on stairs I couldn't love her as Papa—effort to be honest.

School [at Cornwall]. Dread. Fear in school of what "They" would say. Tomboy. Taxidermy. The swamp. Midget [the pony]. Wordsworth. Stars over elm at night. Rabbit tracks in snow. Little Nature my secret companion. . . . Escape to woods and suicide dream, followed by retreat. . . . Cowardice, inhibitive shyness . . .

Helen kept these thoughts to herself and did not know how many others of her age were as lonely and shy as she was. Again and again she wrote about "Little Nature," a fairy child who was her constant companion outdoors, the one perfect friend who understood her thoughts and feelings as no one else did.

Helen's journal was more a workbook than Gretchen's; she used it to probe her own psyche for ideas that could help explain herself to herself and later perhaps be published.

In her last winter at Bryn Mawr School, she had learned a new and comforting way to look at the world, the Indian way. The little girls in the primary class made Indian headbands at Thanksgiving. They wove baskets and molded clay pots. They learned parts of Longfellow's *Song of Hiawatha*; the old Indian grandmother, Nokomis, had answered all of Hiawatha's questions about the moon, the stars, the rainbow, and all the creatures he saw around him—the firefly, "flitting through the dusk of evening, with the twinkle of its candle," the animals and birds who talked their own languages in the great forest "by the shining Big Sea Water."

With the Sherwoods' move to Cornwall, Hiawatha seemed even more like a friend and neighbor. New York State was full of Indian names: Mohawk, Oneida, Onondaga, Cayuga, Seneca—all named for the Five Nations of the Iroquois League, formed by Hiawatha for peace instead of war among the tribes. Helen's high cheekbones gave her an Indian look, which may have pleased her. She began to wear a headband, Indian-style, across her forehead.

Mary's bedtime reading probably included Cooper's *The Last of the Mohicans*. Everyone knew its hero, Uncas, the noble Indian, and Hawkeye, the famous scout whose "feelings appeared to possess the freshness and nature of the forest in which he passed so much of his time." Simple-minded, faithful, utterly without fear, Hawkeye was a character sure to appeal to Helen. He was passionately devoted to the freedom of life in the open and bitterly resented the inroads of the white man's civilization upon the lives and culture of his Indian friends; he was more like an Indian than a white man. Moving swiftly and silently along the forest paths in his moccasins, he nevertheless could not be pushed or hurried against his will. He killed only for food, not for sport.

This was Helen's idea of how life should be lived, and in many ways life at 51 Angola Road was lived Indian-style. Women held a high place there, as they did among the Iroquois; Mary owned the Cornwall farmhouse and was the leader of the Sherwood tribe, as an Iroquois woman owned the longhouse in an Iroquois tribe. Like Indians, the Sherwoods cooked over campfires as soon as the children were old enough to take long hikes through the mountains. A favorite Sherwood winter sport was traveling by snowshoe as the Indians did.

But the Sherwoods had no "braves" at home. Little Sidney, a frail child, remained for a long while a baby in the eyes of his older sisters. They did all the chores that usually would have been shared by the boys in a farm family. Gretchen and Helen taught Jean and Penelope to do the work of stableboys. They fed, stabled, and groomed the horses and ponies. There were always dogs and cats. For a while, a monkey, Mowgli, named for Rudyard Kipling's young boy hero of *The Jungle Books*, was added to the menagerie; Helen loved the Kipling stories because they were full of animals. Mowgli was a rhesus monkey from India, of a breed used for experiments in medical laboratories, and may have been a gift from Uncle Matt, the New York doctor, or

from Dr. Mary in Baltimore. Mowgli was the source of endless fun and endless trouble. Once he walked along a plate
rail and threw all the dishes on the floor. It took time to
clear up the messes made by his mischief, but Helen was
unfailingly patient.

There was never an idle moment at 51 Angola Road. The
chickens had to be fed and their eggs found. In the summer,
the girls weeded the garden. In the winter they shoveled
snow and brought in wood for the fireplace, working as
teams, Gretchen and Penelope, Helen and Jean. After the
morning chores came a quick bath and change of clothes before school. On Saturdays, ashes and cinders from the coal
stove and the furnace had to be spread on the driveway. Saturday was washday too. In the cellar Mary had a hand-
powered machine with a handle that swung back and forth.
The little girls operated it by flinging their weight against it.
Mary rinsed the clothes and hung them on the line while
Mowgli watched. On at least one occasion, he ran along the
clothesline and pulled off all the pins.

When Saturday's chores were done, the young Sherwoods, one by one or with their mother, headed outdoors.
For Helen, this was almost a religious experience, full of
miracles. Spring was a miracle. As she remembered it, "On
certain plants in the fields I found the eggs, cocoons and
chrysalises of many species of moths and butterflies. I kept
them in breeding cages which I made according to specifica-
tions and released the adults after watching them emerge
and dry their wings. The miraculous metamorphosis of many
insects never failed to fill me with wonder and awe." The
year that Helen was twelve, the final dancing school class
was a costume party to which she went as a Promethea
moth, wearing gray flannel pajamas and big waving wings
with red velvet spots added by Mary.

Helen and her animal "museum"

That same year Helen wrote a story for Mamma, "Nature's Fairyland," mixing a little religion, some imagination, and a great deal of close observation from the summer she had spent in the woods and fields and by the pond:

Thousands and thousands of years ago Jesus said, "I am going to put some little fairies on the earth, and some of them shall teach man how to sing, and some shall teach him how to weave, and some shall teach him how to work . . . and man will love and protect them."

So first He made a little creature which was black and white with a little yellow cap on his head. . . . When he was made Jesus said to him, "Thou shalt fly high up into the air and while thou art flying thou shalt sing this song. . . ." When the people on the earth heard the song they thought it was an angel coming down from heaven. . . . And they took it

in their hands and cried, "O, who are you, and where did you
come from? O sing again, sing, sing again!"

Young Francis of Assisi, singing of Brother Sun and All
His Creatures, might have written something like this in a
moment of ecstatic joy. A friend of Gretchen's, whom she
called "Uncle Harry," once told her that he expected Helen
to turn into a kind of saint.

Today, Helen's story sounds naive, but Mary kept it
among her treasures. Two years later, Helen was fifteen
when Prue Ellis came for Thanksgiving and wrote home that
all of the Sherwoods were naive; that was part of their
charm. Helen was different from anyone Prue had ever met.
"She is very reserved with people," Prue wrote, "but when
she talks in her low deep voice she says things worth hearing." As Gretchen said in her journal, the best people always
saw something fine in Helen.

No one had more sympathy for animals. Remembering
her childhood at Cornwall, she wrote, "In winter, there
were animal tracks in the snow, especially rabbits and crows.
In early spring thaws, piles of stone and earth were apt to
appear where woodchucks started their remarkable spring
house cleaning. . . ." When Helen was fifteen, *The Wind in
the Willows* was published and Mary read it aloud. It became a family favorite with its opening chapter on Rat's
spring cleaning; Helen understood perfectly how Mole and
Ratty, Badger and Toad lived and felt.

Helen lacked many of her mother's skills, but she had in-
herited clever hands, and Bryn Mawr School had given her
an early start in handicrafts; the primary children learned to
saw and file and nail and paint. While Gretchen was in college, the ceiling of the big upstairs bedroom started to fall
after ninety years of service. Mary decided to pull down the

plaster and nail fresh beaverboard between the exposed wooden beams. This was the room where all four girls slept, each in her own corner. With Mary as boss, Helen headed the work crew of her sisters, knocking down plaster and throwing it over the railing of the upstairs porch. Sidney had a little sledge; with Gypsy the pony pulling, the plaster was hauled away and dumped on the driveway. By nightfall the big bedroom was finished and looked attractive enough for any Vassar guests who might come. Later when Helen took up weaving and had a big loom in that upstairs room, Mary learned to weave. When Helen took up pottery, Mary learned at her side.

But even with all of Helen's skills, being different was painful. In a journal she kept in later years, she wrote that she had had no one, neither child nor adult, with whom she could share her inmost thoughts and interests. Gretchen-and-Helen, as the family called them, were never really a pair. Gretchen had already finished her junior year at college by the time Helen was in her last months of high school and working on her final required paper, "The Birds of Cornwall." Science and math were her best subjects, but she needed some tutoring to make sure of passing her college entrance examinations. Probably the whole family as well as her tutor sensed that college would be a strain for Helen.

As she got ready for Vassar in the fall of 1911, her mother was facing college expenses for two daughters; Gretchen would be a senior that year. Helen had few clothes except the simple ones needed for attending high school at Cornwall, doing chores, tending animals, and hiking in the mountains. Family pictures show the Sherwood children well dressed by today's casual standards; fifty years later, Helen would have lived in blue jeans and been in style, but coming from the country to Vassar in 1911 with homemade clothes, she may have had some pangs.

There is no way to know whether she would have been interested in clothes if she had been brought up differently, but it is unlikely that she would ever have asked Mamma for a party dress to wear to a college dance. She knew how to dance, but it is not certain that she knew a boy whom she could have invited. Mary was careful that her daughters should not be tempted into early marriages with "village boys" whose minds and manners were not good enough, according to her standards. And boys were not the chief interest of the friends Helen made at Vassar. It is hard to picture her dancing at the Junior-Sophomore prom in 1913. Prom weekends could be agony for some girls, if the truth were told. It was an escape to gather up a few friends and head for Cornwall where the home-cooked food was wonderful and the freedom complete.

Helen and her friends were, on the surface, perfectly happy without boys of their own age. One weekend, one of the Vassar guests had to leave for the train to New York. She had been invited by a Yale friend to a party at New Haven and changed into her party dress at 51 Angola Road, while the other girls teased her about leaving all the fun for "some silly boy." What they really felt may have been quite different.

Henry Noble MacCracken, who became president of Vassar in 1915, the year Helen graduated, once wrote an article called "Democracy and the Deviant." He said that a college was a small democracy and that a democracy was "a way of living which emphasized the value of the individual in society." He did not want Vassar to put a "stamp" on its students, so that all would have conventional looks and opinions. He asked, "Is the social pressure at Vassar sufficiently strong to be called a 'stamp'? . . . If this be so, it behooves us to concern ourselves with the individuals who do not subscribe to these views and who seek for themselves a different orientation. . . . Intellectual deviation is that which I have most at heart."

Deviants came in all sizes and styles, and President Mac-Cracken wanted all to feel comfortable at Vassar as long as they graduated with a worthwhile purpose in life. Some did. During Helen's junior year, a recent graduate, Inez Milholland, led a suffrage parade of a thousand women through the nation's capital. She was wearing a white Cossack suit, white kid boots, and a pale blue cloak embroidered with a gold cross. She was mounted on a white horse. Inez was one of President MacCracken's "deviants" who had found a purpose in life.

Helen Sherwood's style was the opposite; when she mounted a horse, she took off for the solitude of the woods. She would never have ridden past the White House with a thousand women parading after her. When she graduated she had not found a purpose in life, and she would not have been voted "the girl most likely to succeed."

Her notebooks recorded stressful memories of college: "Felt power but never shared or expressed thoughts. Some day, Nature and I against the wicked world. . . . Mamma's ideal—Papa. Only one love—always in future, no effort on my part. Fate and my lover would claim me. Fear of inadequacy. Infantile emotion. . . ."

If Helen had only known it, many other girls at Vassar suffered from the same doubts and fears, no matter how sophisticated they looked. But she had no way of knowing. Perhaps no college could have met the needs of her teenage years. One of her friends, remembering her in college, has written, "I can think of classmates, her peers, who might have been sensitive enough to rate Helen properly." But there were not many. Girls with the "Vassar stamp" may not have troubled to look twice at Helen in her plain

Helen at Vassar

homemade clothes or to wonder what lay beneath her quiet reserve. A few did. The same friend writes: "I have before me in the 1915 *Vassarion* a charming picture of Helen Sherwood as a senior, thoughtful, withdrawn, quite beautiful." The caption under her picture reads: "People who are chuck plumb full o'thoughts haven't time to take it out in talking."

Later, Helen wrote of her Vassar experience: "Self—had the interests, eyes and curiosity as well as drawing and painting ability (copying) of a Naturalist. . . . Also descriptive writing ability. Also interest in teaching Nature Study to children. Since college—have been groping. World is not ideal. Want to put my ideas across to 'blind' world. . . . College gave us picture of 'blindness' of world. Made us missionaries but took away simple natural heritage of every woman to live life to full and enjoy it, developing own personality and interests in natural ways."

After graduation, in the summer of 1915, she went, perhaps with a friend, to Woods Hole on Cape Cod, Massachusetts. There, one day, at the Marine Biological Laboratory, she watched under a microscope what seemed to her a miracle. It was science and it was poetry. Her journal said:

JULY 6, 1915 . . . I have watched, with a very childlike wonder, the coming to life of a creature. It is sublime beauty that I have seen, the process of creation has been unfolded before me. I have watched the mingling of the sperm and ovum and seen the strange, magic spindle form and vanish. I have seen the cleavage of one cell into two with indescribable delicacy of action, and into many cells, which by some unknown guiding, moved about and gathered together and showed themselves in dark lines and humps and formed an ever growing ring that traveled round the egg leaving a film of cells behind it.

At length a long dark hump, thickened at one end, slowly took shape, until a head was dimly marked out, then a neck, a long, snaky body, and tiny somites at either side. This little, naked thing of transparent stuff kept forming and rising from a strange, changing, moving mass of cells, and its tiny head with bulging eyes startled me as I recognized it. Then little clusters and branching lines arranged themselves on the egg surface, a tiny quivering caught my eye, and I saw the heart of this minute creature beat its first beat. This little sea-child that was being born lay like a tiny thread on the yolk of an egg that I could scarcely see unmagnified. O Science, I cried, you have revealed creation to me. I ask of you one thing. Whatever caused that first shiver of life leave undiscovered that we may still imagine, and poetry may be born.

Could her mission in life be teaching nature study to children, finding ways to teach that would let her share her own intense joy? But following the ecstatic experience at Woods Hole, and having begun to teach with high hopes, came two years of unmitigated disaster.

Among the crises of her life, Helen listed two that immediately followed college: "Arlington—Vancouver. Fired from first two positions as teacher of children. My ideal, to teach children of [about] Nature." Arlington may have been the village on the edge of the familiar Vassar campus; Vancouver was on the unfamiliar and distant Pacific coast of British Columbia. There is no record of why Helen failed. Perhaps, like Gretchen, she was unable to keep up with the pressure of the work. Perhaps she seemed strange; sometimes she thought so herself. She wrote about this crushing double blow as if it had happened to another young girl: "She was an idealist. She had spent her childhood as a self-taught naturalist, developing a passionate love and knowledge of nature. On graduating from college she strode forth into the world with her head in the clouds and her heart set upon teaching the world to see and love the beauty and wonder of Nature. She was rebuffed and pushed aside by the sophisticated world who scorned to look at her vision. The blindness and hardness she confronted, and then the war, threw her into a profound depression and terrifying, fantastic visions took possession of her mind. For months she lived in a world of nightmares conjured up by her uncontrolled and vivid imagination. . . ."

Helen went home from Vancouver to recuperate. Probably she helped Mamma at the Red Cross workroom in Cornwall, but much of her free time was spent in writing lyrical descriptions and philosophical meditations on life and on mankind's willful destruction of natural beauty. Her suffering was so obvious that Dr. Mary was called on for help. She took Helen with her to Baltimore and arranged for her to have treatment of a new kind, called occupational therapy.

At this time, soldiers were returning from combat with wounded minds as well as wounded bodies. A National Association of Physical Therapists had been organized in the United States, largely for the benefit of the veterans, and rehabilitation centers were being set up throughout the country. The aim at first was simply to find new occupations by which handicapped men could earn a living. Then psychiatrists began to order occupational therapy for other patients brooding over nightmarish horrors, real or imagined. Anyone trapped in such misery could benefit.

Actually, neither psychiatry nor occupational therapy was new. Mental illness was as old as mankind, and there had always been ways to treat it, some of them harsh and even cruel. But by about 1860, psychiatrists were working on the humane theory that the mentally ill were normal people who had undergone more social and psychological stress than they could bear. From 1920 onward, Helen used her journal as a way to exorcise the troublesome ghosts of her past.

She wrote: "I was always clinging to an idealistic, mid-Victorian mother. Still do. Sex urge strong but repressed. Not mature. Uncle Matt not consciously masculine to me. . . . Fun, camping, building—more like boy, son. Drawn to men but ungracious, unappreciative, unreceptive of attentions. Why was this? Did I try to be a boy? Why? Mamma's immature understanding of daughters, young girls. Strictness, emphasis on work, and walking. Why? Perhaps she repressed her sex urge, walking. Did not dare relax. Perhaps I longed most, as a child, for gentleness, beauty of color, peace of thoughts. Little Nature and I. Fixated for years at 12 year level. What level now? What resentments still carried? . . . Intense desire for children and home of my own. . . . Mamma—developed passion for attainment and fame—Papa's life carried on through us—blinding her to our human desires. . . . Me—clinging, longing, lacking self-confidence but wanting independence. Stubborn, idealistic, imaginative, queer. Wanting a husband *and* my independence."

Probing the wound may have been helpful to some extent, though Helen was to be subject to periods of self-doubt and depression as long as she lived.

Yet it was Helen, perhaps more than any other of her children, who shared with Mary moments of ecstasy. The preface to Mary's autobiography tells how her religious faith was restored:

JANUARY 24, 1925. The eclipse of the sun (total). Helen and I went to the Cornwall Hill to watch. We got there on snowshoes at 8 a.m., thermometer 10 degrees below zero. The shadow was just beginning. . . . As the shadow covered the sun fully, there was a beautiful halo of rainbow colors in the deep blue sky, a brilliant corona with irregular spikes of light. The planets Venus, Mercury and Jupiter, the marvelously clear atmosphere, all outlined most vividly the surrounding mountains; Schunemunk, the Beacons, Storm King and Black Rock. The yellow, pink, and green colors in the sky and the white carpet of snow! It seemed "The Glorification of Light"!

For the second time in my life, I believed absolutely in the existence of a God who controls all things. . . . That Power, I bow before, believe in and like to call "Father." The Power that controls the Sun, and Moon, the Stars, yes, and our lives.

Helen's experience with occupational therapy was totally satisfying. Patients were offered a wide selection of crafts and could choose freely from basketry, leather work, weaving, wood work, and a dozen others. Helen's hands were clever and experienced. As she worked, a real healing of mind took place. The therapists who helped her were young, kind, tactful, patient, and interested. They had, in fact, all her own qualities of personality. Before she had finished her course of treatment, she had found her calling, her cause. She wanted to be an occupational therapist, working in a hospital for wounded soldiers.

She began by serving a four-year apprenticeship at a workshop called Snow-Abbott Looms in New York City, and during the summers had at least one pupil at 51 Angola Road, who remembers those days as a wonderful experience: "Helen set up a workshop in the little log cabin in the garden and one summer (or two) when I was nine or ten I spent several mornings a week there with her. She taught me to weave on one of the small table looms she had there, and we worked on various nature crafts, gathering sweetfern on our mountain hikes for sachets or to line small painted boxes. Helen was a kind, warm person and it was a very peaceful companionable relationship we shared—a bond that lasted till I grew up and went away. I think it was a happy time for both of us—the bees buzzed in the hollyhocks outside the small open casement windows, and the scent of the warm grasses blew in from the meadows beyond. . . ."

It was a healing time for Helen. Aunt Margaret helped to ease the financial strain during this period when Helen's earnings were small and at times nonexistent. Her account book for the years 1917 to 1923 shows nineteen gifts to the Sherwood children, eleven of them for Helen.

By 1927 Helen had decided on what was to be a vital step forward. She enrolled for a two-year course as a student in the Boston School of Occupational Therapy, probably with financial help and encouragement from Aunt Margaret and Dr. Mary. Jean was married, living at Natick, Massachusetts, an easy train ride from Boston; she and her husband made Helen a part of their family for the two years. Founded in 1918 "to meet the war-time need," the school had grown and was setting high standards in this new profession. It maintained a clinic and received patients from doctors and hospitals, giving the students practical experience. "Craft instruction is an essential part of the course," read the school's brochure. "But here the patient's reaction, both physical and mental, and the improvement it effects in his condition, are the essential factors to be considered by the student therapist." This seemingly simple and sound principle was to prove a controversial one when Helen went out into "the real world" as a licensed occupational therapist, but for the moment, she was blissfully happy. She wrote a note for a 1915 Vassar reunion newsletter: "I am thrilled every minute as I never was thrilled before." She had found a cause to which she could give her life, and perhaps equally important, she had moved from a woman's world to a world of men.

By 1932 she was established as occupational therapist at the Rockland State Hospital in Orangeburg, New York. Her specialty was teaching the art of weaving Oriental-style rugs, and she used the hospital garden as therapy for her patients; they found new hope in watching fresh life spring up from small brown seeds and ugly bulbs that they themselves had planted and tended. She brought in pets, following the recommendation of Sigmund Freud. For some mysterious reason, pets were often more helpful than any human aid; they gave, in Freud's words, "affection without any ambivalence, a feeling of close relationship, of undeniably belonging together." A pet to love and be loved by, a pet that did not criticize, did not judge, a pet that needed daily care, worked magic. It would be fifty years before institutions for the mentally ill would seriously use pets in therapy, with research to prove their value; Helen Sherwood was among the first to introduce the idea in a hospital.

She devoted herself wholeheartedly to her patients,

whether or not they were the veterans she had wanted to serve; she made notes about some in whom she was especially interested: "Walter. Weaving feverishly as an escape from regrets and self-pity—long periods of depression. Later—dancing. Jimmy. Wood carving—almost mute and very inert. Later—learned to dance and became sociable. Raymond. Catatonic. Weaving when almost mute and inert. Later—dancing and athletics. Harry. Psychoneurotic. Wood carving. Sigmund—emotionally dead. Exciting colors. [Made trip to] Madison Square Garden. Henry and Bernard. Manic boys and model ships—attention to fine details, using patience impossible in other work tried. Rabinowitz and Oriental rug."

In therapy, all occupations should have a meaning beyond the work itself, and Oriental rug patterns were a dramatic example. Helen wrote an article, hoping that it might interest the new *Occupational Therapy Magazine*. She described her final conversation with "the first patient in a state of manic excitement I had ever supplied with work on an Oriental rug." Now she felt a thrill of pleasure at his appearance.

He was a small, alert, quick-witted man of 40 or so, with kind, keen, laughing eyes and a sociable smile. He was carefully and smartly dressed, and his manner was courteous and polished. A sudden mental picture of the same man two months ago in contrast to his appearance today was the cause of my thrill of pleasure. Perhaps the same picture passed before his mind, for he said, "I behaved dreadfully for a while, didn't I? Swearing, protesting, making all the noise and annoyance I could. . . . I am so sorry and I want to apologize. . . . Guess what first started me back on the right track; it was one word you kept using every time I lost the place in my pattern. . . . You used to say, so patiently and confidently, "When you learn to *visualize* the pattern, you will not lose your place." You used to take the chart and hold it off at a distance. "Look at it," you would say. "Not at each separate square of color, but visualize the design as a whole." Something about the idea seemed to ring true. . . . The details that had confused me so took their proper perspective and fitted right into the picture automatically. . . . Then I got well in a hurry. You see, I applied the same principle to myself. . . .

Helen continued, "I am relating his experience simply as an interesting application by him of a principle of craft work to his personality problem. . . . As it is the tendency of the manic type of personality to be distracted and confused by exacting details, [occupational therapy] should produce a similar result, providing the patient with a new and lasting interest and with a safeguard he might utilize whenever he felt himself losing his perspective."

This report may never have been published; it was followed in Helen's journal by a list of other patients: Clayton, Keifer, Junda, Saboe, Shipley, Tony, Serafinas, Burits, Alfred, Robert, Seth, Pedolka, Bob, Huff.

Helen touched the lives of many patients during her years at Rockland. At long last, at the age of thirty-eight, she had found a place in the world where she was needed and was effective. With the ending of World War II, more and more soldiers were coming back to hospitals. It was then, at the age of fifty-one, after thirteen years at Rockland, that Helen wrote a letter of resignation to the supervisor, a foolish move for a woman who needed badly to have a job that she could count on, but her reasons were important: "I know I have something to contribute to the neuropsychiatric soldiers [in a veterans hospital run by the federal government] because of my training, experience and desire to help them. I shall not be satisfied until I am helping them."

Her second reason was a criticism: "I am taking this opportunity to tell you how I have felt for many years about New York State psychiatric occupational therapy. Very few of the heads of occupational therapy departments are graduates of occupational therapy schools. . . . It is almost humanly impossible for them not to prefer an untrained to a trained personnel to supervise." These supervisors were very proud of the sales rooms where the work of the patients advertised the hospitals' occupational therapy programs and brought in a good profit. But this should not be the purpose of the work; it was the patient's welfare that counted. "Whether what he makes is saleable or not is aside from the point. Occupational therapy is only the first step toward developing in him a *personality* adequate to go out and make a living in the world." Helen described a veterans' hospital as she expected it to be: "A patient ready to leave an occupational therapy class is not simply put to work mopping the dining room floors, for instance, and then lost sight of. Because he is a good mopper and badly needed, he is not kept at this work after it ceases to benefit him. He is constantly moved up from simple to more responsible jobs until he is ready for parole."

This was how things should be done but could not be done at Rockland even if their policy were changed. The Rockland hospital was so short staffed that Helen was spending most of her time doing the duties of a nurse's aide; World War II had drained away most of the younger therapists for duty overseas. Occupational therapy on the home front suffered. The superintendent tried to persuade Helen not to leave. He needed her, and he was sure that she would not like the rules and regulations of a veterans' hospital run by the federal government, but at last he let her go. She went to work in the big veterans' hospital at Coatesville, Pennsylvania.

Helen had often quoted an old Irish adage, "'What will

you have?' quoth God. 'Pay for it and take it.'" She paid for
her new job at the Coatesville veterans' hospital by losing
her old job at Rockland, and the new job failed to fulfill her
hopes. On April 16, 1945, four days after the death of President Roosevelt and not quite a month before Germany sur-
rendered to the Allies, she drafted a letter to the
superintendent of the veterans' hospital on behalf of patients, many of whom had been disabled during combat:
"Many have faced dangers no one but a soldier can conceive
of. . . . Any man who has had the courage to fight in this
ghastly war, including those who broke early under the
strain, have a right to the best treatment by the most coura-
geous government employees." Instead, Helen found at
Coatesville executives who were afraid to allow work and
recreation outdoors because of the risk that patients might
escape. The hospital offered no treatment except physical
therapy and shock treatment. There was no gym. The swimming pool was not used. There was no ball park, no farm.
There were no tools or other equipment for occupational
therapy. Many patients felt humiliated when they were
given work that was far beneath their intellectual level and
interests.

By contrast, Helen looked back at the humane and effective work she had been allowed to do with disturbed male
patients at Rockland: "I have had victory gardens and farm
work, and shops of 25–35 patients using carpentry tools. I
have never had any serious accidents in the shops, and the
few patients who have eloped from the garden and farm have
been found shortly. It was recognized by the executives that
the risk was small compared with the benefits. [There is a
fear] that if a patient is not found, the employee losing him
may lose his job. This never worried me. I was there to help
the patients, and have a strong faith in nature's curative

powers out-of-doors. There is need of immediate action before their disease has progressed beyond our power to help. . . ."

There is no record of whether or not Helen sent this letter to the superintendent at Coatesville. She stayed there for two years. It is not known whether she resigned or was fired.

Briefly, she worked at St. Vincent's Retreat in Harrison, New York, coming home for weekends and putting a good face on things outwardly, but inwardly fighting off despair. Only Mamma and Penelope were at home now. Gretchen was living in Washington, working as senior translator in the State Department and spending her vacations in France; both Jean and Sidney were married and gone. All of them were settled in the world; why not Helen? She had reached for the highest good and only fallen, again and again. What, really, was the difference between a saint and an idiot, she wondered.

She bought a new notebook and filled page after page with her distress but never showed it openly. Mamma failed to see, and Helen was astounded: "The other day Mamma used the word placid in describing me! Mamma—who sometimes sees through all my camouflage, and 'placid' of all qualities repulsive and—I hope—inapplicable to me in any mood. It gave me a deep shock. My shell of camouflage, my defensive wall, my protective coat of indifference, my self-built prison wall must be escaped from. The fire of my soul must have free air. As I try to open the doors of my patients' cages, I myself must live in freedom. . . . Within each human being is such wonderful joy and beauty and love and creative power *imprisoned*. . . ." In 1956 Helen returned to work at the Rockland hospital.

In 1961 both job and introspection ended suddenly. They

no longer mattered. Gretchen had resigned from her Washington job and had gone to live permanently in Céreste. She
was working on a book about the Crusades when her health
failed and she learned that she had lung cancer. She had
been a chain smoker for many years; both Helen and Penelope stopped smoking at this time. In March Helen went to
be with Gretchen at the hospital in Aix-en-Provence. No job
commitments held her back, and she had always been the
one closest to Gretchen. There were "excellent weeks of
convalescence, including fighting cobalt therapy, hopes and
plans for life in Céreste. Then jaundice, at first apparently
simple. The first week in May complete bed rest ordered.
Slow but gradual improvement, return of severe symptoms,
sudden aggravation of severe symptoms, no hope. Semi-
conscious days. Coma. The end, Sunday afternoon, July 2.
Was she aware of the end, concealing her awareness from
me, while I, as the doctor wished, made every effort to con-
ceal my knowledge from her?"

Nature was her most beautiful during those weeks: "Each
day the wide fields, the hills and mountains and every roadside changed their flowery garments. . . . Around Céreste,
in April, acres and acres of poet's narcissus in all the low
meadows, perfuming the magic air. . . . Flowers of every
tone and shade of purple and lavender and rose, of pale
and deep yellow, of variety and subtlety and delicacy and
vividness beyond words. Fragrance everywhere in the inde-
scribably, subtly luminous, rapt atmosphere of Provence—
Cézanne's Provence," still unspoiled. She had brought
flowers to Gretchen every day.

Yet Provence was no more beautiful than the Hudson
River valley, which was so much younger in human history
and was already threatened by plans for industrial development and superhighways. When Helen came home from

France, she felt sick at the sound of trucks roaring along the river roads, of bulldozers tearing up flowery fields and wooded mountainsides, uprooting the homes of little creatures that had lived there. She kept bees and began to raise Angora rabbits. Her journal now had a new emphasis. She was possessed with the idea that modern man had lost his ancient place in the scheme of nature through his greed for power and for things. "Things are in the saddle / And ride mankind," Emerson had said a hundred years ago. It was far more true now.

Over Cornwall loomed a special threat. Consolidated Edison, known as Con Ed, a mammoth utilities company based in New York City, had already drawn up plans to build a power plant at Storm King Mountain. (Cornwall would be a suitable place to build, said Con Ed; it had no historic importance, there was nothing there to spoil.) Outraged residents were forming an organization called Scenic Hudson to stop the project. Lawyers had to be hired, telegrams had to be rushed to state legislators at Albany. There must be an election of officers, meetings, publicity launching an ongoing effort for as long as it might take to stop Con Ed.

What Con Ed proposed was to construct a storage plant for pumping water uphill to the top of Storm King, where a reservoir would hold the water until times when extra power was needed, then release it back down past turbines generating electricity. Con Ed petitioned that such a plant would give New York City efficient, pollution-free, and economical energy for emergencies.

Environmentalists and many scientists alike were violently opposed. What of the effect on Storm King, and the Hudson itself, that majestic sweep of mountain and river engraved on the Earth by the last Ice Age? America the Beautiful! And it was at this point, of all places, that Con Ed proposed to raise a concrete tailrace with abutments 32 feet high and 685 feet long. This would be the new view of Storm King from the river. Even worse, brackish Hudson River water in the proposed reservoir could pollute the fresh water table in the mountains, including the Cornwall reservoir. Naturalists from five states protested too; once Storm King's pumps began to churn, fish with their eggs and larvae would be killed as they were forced uphill through a two-mile tunnel, or suffocated in the silt-filled reservoir. Wildlife in the mountain forest would vanish.

The cost of the project had trebled even before a shovel could be sunk in the mountain, but Con Ed was prepared to spend whatever was needed. Scenic Hudson started with a few thousand dollars and the volunteer help of a few friends and neighbors. One of them was Helen Sherwood. She scraped together every cent she could afford to give, and more that she could not afford; she became the secretary of the little group. It was David against Goliath.

Their case went to court in 1965 and a judge ruled that concerned citizens had the right to be heard. They struggled on. A group of Vassar classmates from 1915 met regularly at an apartment in New York City; Helen was often there and they talked about Con Ed and Storm King. One of them has written: "Most of us were born under the spell of the Hudson and the Palisades and joined Helen's concern. She had matured into a dignity, a presence we had perhaps sensed in the college days. Now she was released ardently to another Cause and she could fight effectively."

In October 1971, a *New York Times* article listed organizations that had joined Scenic Hudson: the Sierra Club, the Wilderness Society, the Izaak Walton League, the National Audubon Society, the National Parks and Conservation Association, the Hudson River Conservation Society. What had begun as a trickle was now a flood. The *Times* article was headed: "New Moves Are Planned to Bar Con Edison's Storm King Plan."

Helen Sherwood recorded everything that was said or done on both sides of the controversy. Eventually, dozens of large cardboard boxes were filled with the records of the great fight. In 1982, on the day before the celebration of Franklin Delano Roosevelt's hundredth birthday, the Storm King papers were given to the library at Hyde Park built and named in his memory.

The Storm King papers were impressive. They recorded that in 1982 Con Ed officially transferred title to twenty acres of riverfront land to the village of Cornwall-on-Hudson for recreational use and four hundred acres of woodland to the Palisades Interstate Park Commission. A Hudson River Foundation was being created for independent research on river issues, such as pollution, and plans for two other industrial plants along the river were halted when Con Ed gave up the Storm King project.

On request, anyone can study the papers, which have made the Roosevelt Library a major center for records of the efforts over many years to preserve the natural beauty and heritage of the Hudson River. The papers are filed under "Storm King" with a cross-reference under "Sherwood, Helen." Like a moth coming out of its chrysalis, Helen had won for herself a kind of immortality.

Another lasting memorial of Helen's work is the Museum of the Hudson Highlands, a rustic stone-and-wood building in the shadow of Storm King. Here children and adults come all year round to see exhibits of the animals and birds that live in the woods. Visitors follow the nature trails, learning about the ancient origins of the Hudson and its mountains, and about the life of the Iroquois and Algonquin Indians who once lived there. Helen, who looked like an Indian and had always wanted to teach nature study, was one of the founders of the museum. She offered the twelve acres of the old farm at 51 Angola Road to be kept as she had known it from childhood. It was a great disappointment to her that the museum could not accept the gift.

People at Cornwall still remember Helen, very slowly driving a small, old car along the road to the museum. One friend wrote about "her wonderful wit and wisdom, her refreshing and sensible outlook and commentary on man's relationship to nature. The trees, the stars, the flowers looked different when she shared through her eyes." And another added: "She was forever the quiet running stream of ideas followed by positive action. This invaluable legacy she leaves for all who knew her well."

She often drove along the high, winding road that skirts the sheer face of Storm King Mountain, and once she pulled her little car off the road, close enough to the rock wall so that she could reach out of the car window and pat that rugged face. It was, after all, a very old friend.

❖ 4 ❖

JEAN

In 1895, Sidney and Mary Sherwood had a child, a boy named Sidney for his father. The baby lived only a few days. The following summer they were expecting another child and rented a nice old farmhouse a mile from the house on Angola Road so that Mary's parents could enjoy four-year-old Gretchen and three-year-old Helen without tiring themselves too much.

The rented house had been built by a Quaker named King Rider, and little Gretchen made up fanciful stories about the expected baby, who would surely be a princess since she would be born in a "King's" house. True enough, the new baby did have the storybook qualities of a princess, being pretty, loving, and lovable. She was named Mary Jean for her maternal grandmother, Mary Jane Beattie, whose "loving, wise, patient, beautiful spirit," in Mary's words, "dominated her life and had been an inspiration to all her children."

Mary Jane died the following spring, and when the Sherwood family came up to Cornwall from Baltimore that summer, they went to the Angola Road house to keep Grandpa Beattie company. An old Cornwall friend, Catherine Westall, helped with the children, and Mary was a conscientious mother, but old Dr. Beattie was not satisfied. He adored the baby, who, in his eyes, was "little Mary Jane come again." He thought that a nursing mother should not be riding a bicycle and taking other strenuous exercise as Mary did. One night when Mary had nursed the baby and gone out to dinner with Sidney, Grandpa Beattie heard the baby crying and carried her out to the cowshed. Catherine Westall found them there. As Mary later wrote, he was "kneeling on one knee with the baby on the other, milking with his free hand while the baby held her mouth open like a little bird, catching the stream of milk. Catherine called: 'Why, Doctor, what are you doing?' Father replied: 'The baby was crying. She was hungry. Her mother should not neglect her as she does.'"

Jean was not neglected. Her parents loved her dearly, and her childhood memories were happy. In the fall, the family returned to Baltimore, where Sidney's seminar students made a pet of her but teased him by calling his third girl "Diminishing Utility," as if she had been some sort of factor in political economy.

Many years later, she recorded her childhood memories. "I am not writing for any particular reading audience," she wrote. "He who runs, may read." She would have liked to put it all into a poem. "Life to me, as far back as I can remember, has always been poetically thrilling. . . ." But she put it into prose.

One vivid little recollection (I can still feel the warmth and strength of that hand)—we were in Cornwall, I suppose in

Jean at about the age of four

the summer of 1900, and Papa and I were walking to the village. Apparently he was in a hurry, for just outside the stone wall, he took my hand and, bending his head to speak down to me, said gently and understandingly "Am I walking too fast for you?" I answered quickly in the negative. . . . I can still feel the tenderness in Papa's mellow voice.

The only other incident I remember clearly occurred about that time in Baltimore. It was a big event for me. Papa was taking me for the day to the University. Mama was happily sharing my joy in going by dressing me in my best little white dress and blue velvet cape and hat that she had made. I recall looking down proudly at my white socks and shiny black slippers. . . . Again I can feel my own little hand in the safe, warm, firm grasp of my father's as we stepped off the city curb and carefully worked our way through the bustling Baltimore traffic—horses and carriages. My heart was in my mouth at the excitement and danger! Then at the University I [remember] long darkish corridors and tall men talking to Papa and gazing down at me admiringly.

There were memories from Cornwall days: "gardening, plowing with Gypsy; camping and picnicking; skating and coasting; raking leaves and jumping in them; school in Mamma's room with Golda Brown [an old friend of Mary Sherwood] as tutor." Jean was never bored: "cleaning the chicken house every Saturday as I recited 'Horatius at the Bridge'; Mowgli—kerosene lamp [Jean did not say what Mowgli, the pet monkey, did to the kerosene lamp]; telephoning first time, and later still scared to do it; Uncle Matt—building stone walls, the cabin. Mischief, the big tiger tom cat; Bobby, the puppy who went mad and had to be shot; Rossie, the lovely Pierpont Morgan collie."

About 1910, when a member of the Cornwall school board died, Mary Sherwood was asked to take his place and became the first woman to serve on the board. Gretchen was in college, but Mary still had four children in the Cornwall schools and had always been dissatisfied with the school system. No one else seemed to have worried about the dingy, dirty, cold lunchroom in the basement of the elementary school. Mary insisted that the room should be cleaned and the tables and benches painted. A little electric grill was bought so that the children could have a cup of hot soup with their lunch.

Next, Mary helped organize a PTA and became the first secretary. Mothers began to visit the school regularly, meeting the teachers and learning what their problems were. But in the high schools Mary was less successful. She could not persuade the two villages, Cornwall and Cornwall-on-Hudson, to combine their high schools so that they could hire better teachers by paying better salaries. Students who wanted to go on to college still needed to be tutored. A teacher from a private school in Newburgh came once a week to give classes in French, and Golda Brown tutored Jean in Latin. Golda was a talented and popular teacher in Cornwall High School. She came of a Quaker family who introduced the Sherwoods to the Quaker meeting near Angola Road. This influence was to become more and more important to Jean.

With hard work and successful tutoring, she won a four-hundred-dollar state scholarship when she graduated from Cornwall High School. She entered Vassar in September 1914, a month after the outbreak of war in Europe. At first the war seemed remote from the carefree life on college campuses, and President Wilson promised to keep the United States out of the conflict. At Vassar the German Club presented a German nativity play in the chapel, and "Stille Nacht" was sung from the library tower, as always. But in 1916 a sense of disaster hung over Washington and spread throughout the country. German submarines were sighted off the coast of Massachusetts, and when the United States entered the war in April 1917, life changed, most of all for the young.

That summer two hundred girls were organized to work on farms around Poughkeepsie, taking the place of men who had gone to war. Twelve students of outstanding good health and stamina were chosen to run the Vassar farm. Jean was one of the twelve. They roomed and ate together on campus, starting the day at 4:30 A.M. and working for two hours before breakfast. Then came four more hours of work, and after lunch, two more hours. The students earned seventeen and a half cents an hour, with two paid days of vacation each month. They plowed and harrowed fields, planted and weeded vegetable gardens, raked hay, picked berries, made fences, and milked cows. To Jean, the work was nothing new; she enjoyed it.

Despite the war, her college years were happy ones. She made so many friends that she was elected treasurer of her class in her senior year. During the ten years that Mary had daughters at Vassar, more than seventy girls came to Cornwall for weekends, most of them Jean's friends. Mary called them her "adopted daughters" and they called her their "Vassar mother."

Jean was very pretty in her graduation picture for the *Vassarion* of 1918. Her long hair was pinned back, smooth and shining; her eyes and mouth looked ready to smile. The caption read: "Mary Jean Sherwood, Cornwall, New York. Jean, with her beautifully tanned complexion and love of out-doors, was a suitable member of that group of illustrious Vassar farmers last summer. . . . Her lovable personality, however, would make her a welcome member of any illustrious group." She spent two weeks after graduation visiting classmates and then returned to work again on the Vassar farm where she "reveled in every minute of that irresponsible, satisfactory, out-door existence." Responsibility lay in wait. In September she began teaching in the Cornwall-on-Hudson high school. For her first Vassar reunion report she wrote that she was, according to her contract, "responsible for the morals and intellectual development" of forty teenage students to whom she taught biology, physics, and beginning French. "I think I will turn out to be either a minister or a horse trainer! If I'm not preaching manners or morals, I'm applying the horse whip (figuratively, of course!) to these awful 'brats'! (Perhaps the 18-year-old, six-foot boys wouldn't like this title). But there are some interesting features of my

Jean (second from right) with Franklin and Eleanor Roosevelt, Franklin, Jr., John, and Anna at Hyde Park in 1920. Courtesy of Franklin D. Roosevelt Library.

work—interesting new experiences, some very interesting children to work with, my special science, biology, to teach . . . and [I am] hoping in the near future to take up my study of agriculture at Cornell University." She wanted to have a farm of her own.

A year later she was still teaching, still looking forward to studying agriculture at Cornell, and sending warm messages for "anyone of 1918 who comes near Cornwall to remember that the little house on the hill is waiting for you."

Then fate intervened. The following year, 1920, Jean wrote her class note with a new address: "Hyde Park, N.Y. care of Mr. F. D. Roosevelt. My life history since last June has been quite different from what I expected it to be, but in many ways, far more interesting. . . . Suddenly, out of a clear sky, came word from the Vassar College Occupation Bureau that Mr. Franklin D. Roosevelt wanted a tutor for two of his children for the winter. So, within two weeks of the opening of Cornell, I called off all arrangements for an immediate agricultural career, and here I am! Anna, fourteen, and Elliott, ten, are my charges. The work is vitally interesting because I love teaching; the children are fascinating and my experiences interesting in the extreme. . . . Luckily I am a strong Democrat, so my life is safe."

Not too safe, as it turned out, and Jean was not chosen "out of a clear sky." Mrs. Roosevelt herself had conscientiously made the drive to Vassar in search of the perfect tutor for Anna and Elliott. President MacCracken probably played a role in recommending Jean Sherwood as a charming girl with teaching experience, and living nearby. Franklin Delano Roosevelt, Assistant Secretary of the Navy, was campaigning for the vice-presidency with James M. Cox, the Democratic presidential candidate. Mrs. Roosevelt saw it as her duty to go with her husband on the campaign trail, and she paid a price. In her autobiography, *This Is My Story,* she wrote, "I never before had spent my days going on and off platforms, listening apparently with rapt attention to much the same speech, looking pleased at seeing people no matter how tired I was, or greeting complete strangers with effusion." More important, she was anxious about being away from the children.

The five Roosevelt children, too, paid a price for their parents' frequent absences from home. When young James became ill at boarding school, it was his grandmother, Granny Roosevelt, who went to take care of him. After the election, a landslide Republican victory for Warren G. Harding and his running mate, Calvin Coolidge, Franklin and Eleanor

Roosevelt were still constantly on the move from Washington to New York City to Hyde Park and back to Washington. Elliott later wrote in *An Untold Story, the Roosevelts of Hyde Park,* that there was "a complicated living arrangement, devised by Mother, which put Franklin junior, Johnny and their nurse into Granny's town house [in New York] as more or less permanent guests, along with Father. Sis [Anna] and I, with Miss Sherwood, our latest tutor, stayed with Granny in Hyde Park." Eleanor Roosevelt was in New York Monday to Thursday and in Hyde Park Thursday to Monday. The children's father came up from New York for the weekends. A succession of tutors came and went.

Over the years, Granny was the only person who was always at Hyde Park when the children were there; she ruled the roost because it was her nature, and because she felt she had to. Elliott wrote of her motives: "Her son was physically incapable of devoting all the time and attention that growing children need. Her daughter-in-law was obviously bent on building a career for herself at their expense." If Granny thought this, Elliott may have thought so, too, and behaved accordingly. He was "born to trouble as the sparks fly upward." In his mother's words, "He suffered for a great many years with a rather unhappy disposition and I think in all probability I was partly to blame." Elliott was small and sickly. He had to wear braces for a while to correct bowlegs and, as a result, was accident prone. In the middle of a beach picnic, while his parents were sailing, he fell into a bonfire and burned his hands and legs. At the age of six, when his mother had just had another baby, Elliott developed swollen glands and was very ill. From that time until the arrival of Jean Sherwood, the unlucky Elliott often spent weeks in bed. But there was a bright side to bed rest. His mother wrote: "Whatever else it may have done for him, it gave him a taste for books." Jean of course encouraged his reading good books. But he was not easy to handle. James Roosevelt, in *My Parents, a Differing View*, recalled that "Elliott was always the least disciplined of us. When he was three, mother wrote father: 'Elliott bit James hard the other day.'" When he was ten, his disposition had not improved. His mother reported in a letter that Elliott had thrown a kitchen knife at Jean Sherwood. No harm done. "He missed," said James.

(Years later, when the Hyde Park house had been opened to the public, Jean visited it with a group of other tourists. She startled them when she stopped in one room and said loudly and cheerfully, "Oh, this is where Elliott attacked me with the knife!")

Anna, too, had problems. She did not throw knives, but her feelings were in turmoil. "Anna always used to tell me," said Jim Halsted, her third husband, "that her mother was very unpredictable and inconsistent in bringing up her children. Inconsistent in her feelings—sweet and lovely one hour, and the next hour very critical, very demanding, very difficult to be with. You could never quite tell what she really meant."

The peaceful year with Jean had a beneficial effect on Anna. She had thought that her mother did not love her. Now Anna was able to tell her mother that she knew it was not so. Eleanor Roosevelt wrote: "Anna and Elliott loved their winter in the country. They had occasional difficulties with Miss Sherwood which she settled in a very satisfactory manner. Elliott built quite a wonderful dam on one of the little brooks that winter in the lower woods, and around it erected a village and farm. He began collecting flowers and tadpoles to put into the pool created by the dam. . . . It was

a very healthy winter for Anna and Elliott." Jean in fact
made Hyde Park as much like Cornwall as she could. Then,
in Eleanor Roosevelt's account, "In the late spring Miss
Sherwood and Anna had an unfortunate accident. They were
jumping in one of the barns and jumped into what they
thought was a thick pile of hay and found it just a thin layer
over the floor. Both of them broke little bones in their feet
and were laid up for a time." Mary Sherwood must have
been dismayed when she heard of the accident; it was too
much like the day long ago when her brother Frank had hit
his head jumping from a haymow, never to recover.

Several times during the winter of 1920–1921 Jean took
Anna and Elliott home to Cornwall, and Eleanor Roosevelt
and Mary Sherwood became friends. From then on, Mrs.
Roosevelt often drove down with her chauffeur for tea at 51
Angola Road and invited Mary for lunch or dinner at Hyde
Park. Eleanor Roosevelt would send a car to meet Mary at
Poughkeepsie and drive her to Hyde Park, where Jean was
now living almost as one of the family. The grounds were
impressive. They stretched from the main road through an
orchard, past the big house, with a stable, an icehouse, and a
greenhouse clustered around it, and down a long slope of
fields and woods to the Hudson River with a magnificent
view of the Catskill Mountains on the far side. The house
was part fieldstone, part stucco, facing a lawn where pine
trees, scarlet maples, and copper beeches gave shade. The
halls and rooms were spacious, the furniture solid and handsome.

Franklin Roosevelt had taken over a big room at one end
of the house where he could hang his naval paintings and
work on his treasured collections of stamps and coins. Even
more than these, he loved the orchard and woods and hoped
to do experimental plantings to find the right trees for the

Hyde Park soil and climate. On the campaign trail he had seen too many states where serious erosion had already taken place and where farmers were at the mercy of floods and drought. To preserve the beauty and restore the usefulness of American land and waters had become a passion with him, beginning with his own home.

Before Jean left Hyde Park, Franklin Roosevelt asked about her plans for the future. When he heard that she was going to study agriculture at Cornell and hoped to run a fruit farm, he offered her the job of manager of his orchard and woods as soon as she had her degree from Cornell. Here was a golden opportunity, made to order for her. She could look forward to a secure future.

In August 1921 Eleanor Roosevelt invited Jean to bring her mother for two weeks' vacation at Campobello Island off the coast of Maine, where the Roosevelts had two big summer cottages. Mary could not afford such a trip, but Jean used part of her winter's earnings to give her mother this unexpected pleasure. They went by boat to Boston and took the night train to Eastport, Maine, where they were met by the Roosevelts' motorboat and arrived at Campobello early in the morning, just as the family were about to have breakfast. It was a big household that summer: a Scottish housekeeper, a cook, a maid, a gardener, a nurse for Franklin, Jr., and Johnny, the two youngest children, a Williams College student as the new tutor for Jimmy and Elliott, a new French tutor for Anna, and Captain Calder, who was in charge of the launch, boats, and canoes. There were two other guests as well, the wife and small son of Franklin's friend and advisor, Louis Howe. The Sherwoods were introduced to all of these people, but Franklin Roosevelt did not appear. He had arrived at Campobello the day before, very tired, but had decided to take the children swimming. He had then taken a swim by himself in the Bay of Fundy and had run all the way back to the house. Sitting in his wet suit to look at the mail, he began to feel chilly, and went to bed. The day of the Sherwoods' arrival, a doctor was called; he tentatively diagnosed the chill as the start of pneumonia.

Mary and Jean thought that they should help by leaving at once, but Eleanor Roosevelt would not hear of it. Perhaps her husband had nothing more than a heavy cold; he would probably be better in a day or two. The Sherwoods could really help, said their hostess, by taking the older children with their tutors and other guests for some all-day picnics on interesting nearby islands.

Franklin Roosevelt had planned to go himself with the whole party on a three-day camping trip to Lake Utopia, forty miles up the coast, and supplies and food had already been ordered. There was a cabin; they could make mattresses of pine boughs. But by the third day of the Sherwoods' visit, another doctor had to be called in for consultation and it seemed the trip would not be possible. At this point, Mary Sherwood offered to take charge of the expedition, leaving the house at Campobello quiet for the patient. He agreed on condition that "everyone who goes must absolutely obey Mrs. Sherwood and Captain Calder without a question." All drinking water must be boiled.

Someone took a picture of the departure in the well-filled launch; six adults, four children, including little Hartley Howe, whom Mary considered "spoiled," and Anna's big police dog, Chief. Their gear is heaped around them. Elliott is pouting and leans against Jean's shoulder, as if for comfort. She and Captain Calder are the only ones who are smiling. The camping party was not a great success. The weather was bad. The cabin was far from clean. On the third day the party huddled inside, playing endless games, while the rain poured down. And on their return to Campobello they were met with terrible news. Franklin Roosevelt was completely paralyzed in both legs. He had what was then called infantile paralysis, now called polio. Mary and Jean left at once, the most helpful thing they could do.

Jean's path, having led her to the Roosevelts at Hyde Park and Campobello, now took a new turn. Her account of this, written for a class report in 1926, read: "Jean Sherwood Harper (Mrs. Francis Harper) 5 Summit Road, Natick, Mass. My past: Studied agriculture at Cornell '21–'23, and liked it better all the time. Indulged in such frivolities as skiing, cross-country hiking, etc. with a certain interesting person—winter 21–'23,. Acquired an M.S., June 4, 1923 at Ithaca, N.Y. . . ."

The "certain interesting person" was a young man named Francis Harper. He had graduated from Cornell with Phi Beta Kappa honors, served as an officer with the American army in France during World War I, and was working toward a Ph.D. degree in zoology. He had a colorful, even aristocratic family background: a great-grandfather had fought under Wellington at Waterloo, a grandfather had been portrait painter to Maximilian II, King of Bavaria, and a great-grandmother had been lady-in-waiting to Queen Karoline of Bavaria, wife of Maximilian Joseph I. There was a family estate in Ireland. Francis Harper had somewhat aristocratic feelings and an aloofness of manner and spirit that could make barriers between himself and other people. He was tall, handsome, athletic, and he loved the outdoors as much as Jean did. There was a vagabond strain in him. Luxury or even physical comfort meant nothing to him. He had slept on the barren grounds of northern Canada studying animal life, and he had followed the path of the pioneer American naturalist, William Bartram, from the Carolinas down to the swamps of Florida, searching for strange unknown plants; he was fascinated by the people who lived in Georgia's Okefinokee Swamp and talked of going back to study their way of life. Jean adored him. She asked for nothing better than to live wherever Francis wanted to live.

Before her marriage she returned to Hyde Park to tell the Roosevelts about her new plans; later she made a good story of the visit. Franklin Roosevelt was still crippled, as he would be for the rest of his life, using a wheelchair and wearing heavy steel braces on his useless legs, but he was as deep in politics as ever. When she told him why she could not manage the Hyde Park orchards and woods, Jean remembered, "he looked very stern, and scolded me at length for my change of plans [saying] 'No wonder women don't get anywhere—they can't be depended on. I held this job for you for two years and now you choose to get married instead!'" When Jean looked crestfallen at the scolding, he stopped his teasing, laughed at his own joke, and wished her a happy future. She persuaded Francis to send some of his articles on the Okefinokee Swamp to Roosevelt.

Her new life began a few days later, as her Vassar report told the story: "Acquired an M.R.S.—after a severe test of self-possession for about five minutes, June 14, 1923 at Cornwall, N.Y." The ceremony was almost a duplicate of her mother's wedding. It was not presided over by eight Presbyterian ministers, but Jean and Francis stood on the same Turkoman carpet, laid out on the lawn under the maple trees at 51 Angola Road, where her parents, Mary and Sidney, had stood to be married. Afterward, Jean wrote, she and Francis "went to Michigan by flivver, camping all the way." It was their first taste of years of camping life together. Soon they were camping again, with a grant from the New York State Museum, among the beautiful forests and lakes of the rugged Adirondack Mountains. The result was a hand-book, which they wrote together, on the wild animals of the region.

At the time of her marriage, Jean may not have known that Francis was a man who could not bear supervision. If she had known, she would not have been concerned. But this trait of her husband's was to be an important factor in their lives. Francis liked to apply for grants to do independent research and writing on plants, animals, and conservation. When one grant ended, another had to be found, and there were lean times. Fortunately, a simple way of life suited both Francis and Jean, but there would not be much security.

Looking back years later, Jean wrote an essay for the "I Personally" essay contest, sponsored by the *Atlantic Monthly*. It was as if she had to share a secret with the world, to make public the "joy and satisfaction untold . . . when living in the utmost simplicity from a materialistic point of view." She wrote: "For about six years our road led smoothly on, up hill, down dale; sun-flecked, rain-drenched—we loved it all. . . . *How* we have worked! *How* we have loved, *how* we have lived!"

The Harpers' first child, named Mary Sherwood for her grandmother, and called Molly, was born in 1926. Robert Francis, called Robin, arrived two years later. "Encumbrances?" said their mother. "Hardly ever, for they, too, loved the rough and simple life from babyhood. Camping for longer or shorter periods, to make careful studies of the wildlife of certain areas, form the highlights of those early years." One of these areas was the great Georgia swamp, called by the Indians "the Okefinokee, land of the trembling earth." Francis was outraged by the lumbering that was going on there. He foresaw that the swamp would soon be destroyed unless Congress took action to stop the damage, but Congress did nothing.

Then came the stock market crash of 1929, followed by the Great Depression. In 1932 Franklin Roosevelt ran for the presidency with the promise of a "New Deal" and was elected in an overwhelming victory. His inaugural address sounded a note of hope and vigor—". . . the only thing we have to fear is fear itself . . ."—but the Depression continued; sixteen million men were now out of work. Roosevelt set up many organizations to put them back to work. One of these organizations was the Civilian Conservation Corps (the CCC), which worked on land reclamation projects all over the United States. Its projects included work on the Okefinokee Swamp.

In 1935 the Harpers were living in Swarthmore, Pennsylvania, while Francis worked for a scientific journal, *Biological Abstracts*, in Philadelphia, coming and going by train; the Harpers owned no car. Swarthmore College had been founded by the Society of Friends, the Quakers. The town was a center for numerous groups that promoted Quaker principles. Jean joined the Women's International League for Peace and Freedom with which she was to work as a volunteer for the next thirty years, and she became deeply committed to the Quaker faith. But life in Swarthmore could not continue. In 1935, when the Harpers' third child, Lucy Lee, was only two years old, *Biological Abstracts* had to cut its staff, and Francis lost his job. He and Jean had saved a little money, but it was absolutely necessary to find a place where they and their children could live on the smallest possible amount of money until another grant turned up.

Francis had once planned to write a book called *The Okefinokee Folk*, which would be a record of the animals and plants of the swamp. Later it was also the life of its people that he loved—the way they talked, the stories they told, the music they played and sang, the things they believed. Now, with the end of the Depression nowhere in sight, he might write this book. Jean said, "With high hopes, we bought an old Ford, stored our worldly goods, and set out on our thousand-mile trek. We went by easy stages, camping all the way, and finally arrived at the little cabin we had engaged to rent near Folkston, Georgia, on the outskirts of the Okefinokee Swamp."

In William Bartram's day, late in the eighteenth century, the Creek Indians had believed that there was a mysterious island somewhere in the swamp, "a most blissful spot of the earth." Bartram told in his *Travels* that sometimes Creek hunters, hopelessly lost in the swamp, would find the island, just as they were about to perish. "Beautiful women, whom they called daughters of the sun . . . kindly gave them such provisions as they had with them, which were chiefly fruits, oranges, dates, &c. and some corn cakes. . . . They further say, that these hunters had a view of their settlements, situated on the elevated banks of an island, or promontory, in a beautiful lake; but that in their endeavors to approach it, it seemed to fly before them, alternately appearing and disappearing. . . ." Other young warriors would try to find the island, but in vain, though they often came upon strange canoes and the footprints of men who must have come from that paradise.

On the real islands of the Okefinokee there was danger as well as beauty. Along the shores, alligators lay as still as fallen trees, half in, half out of the water, or submerged, only their eyes and nostrils showing. There is a picture of Molly, Robin, and Lucy contemplating a bear that has just been shot, and another of three-year-old Lucy patting a dead wildcat that sits, stiff, propped up, but looking quite at

home, on a cabin porch. Venomous water moccasins took
their rest on branches overhanging the swamp, and it was
wise to look before stepping over logs; diamondback rat-
tlesnakes liked to sun themselves there. They could be six to
eight feet long but were less dangerous than the bright,
pretty little coral snake whose bite caused paralysis and, possibly, death. There were swarms of mosquitoes.

Even so, Jean felt at once the magic of the Okefinokee
about which Francis cared so much. Its lakes and creeks
were almost black with the tannic acid from cypress boles.
The surface of the water shone like a mirror, making double
images above and below, so that a small boat seemed to
move through the sky between trees that grew right side up
and upside down, hung with gray Spanish moss. In the narrow creeks, smaller trees closed in so that a boat slid through
a green tunnel. In some places one came upon open water
"prairies" often choked with lush growth of lilies and other
aquatic plants.

The air was full of birdsong. Francis found more than a
hundred kinds of birds in the swamp and learned the names
given to them by the people who lived there. The great blue
heron was "po' jo," "po' Job," or "the preacher"; the pileated
woodpecker was "the lord-God" or "good-God"; the wren,
"the fence dodger" or "shaky bag." At night the weird shriek
of the "skritch owl" was added to the deafening chorus of
frogs. Francis would go to any amount of trouble to satisfy
his scientific curiosity about the swamp creatures. One night
when he and Jean were chugging along in their old car on a
dark road at the edge of the swamp, the noise of the engine
and the din of the croaking frogs filled the woods. "Suddenly," as Jean remembered, "Francis stopped the car,
grabbed his flashlight and disappeared into the moccasin-
infested swamp." He was gone for almost two hours while

Jean sat alone in the darkness. When he finally reappeared, he was holding something in his hands and looking very happy. "Among the croaks of thousands of other frogs and above the roar of the motor in his car, his sensitive ear had detected the notes of the bird-song frog which never before had been found in that part of the United States, a specimen of which he captured and brought back with him."

The human inhabitants of the swamp came from Scotch-Irish pioneer ancestors who had found their way into the Okefinokee, liked the carefree life, and settled there. They were proud to call themselves "Crackers," the old Scottish word for an independent person; they were proud that they could get along without the material things that most people thought they had to have for happiness. But outsiders looked down on Crackers as poor, uneducated, ignorant, of no account. When Francis Harper first came to the Okefinokee, he was amused by the Crackers' primitive ways and kept notebooks of their unique dialect with its special vocabulary. When he returned with Jean, and later with their children, his feeling for the Crackers had grown to respect, admiration, and deep affection. In spite of their poverty, they were superlative friends, in his words, "genial, warm-hearted, and generous to an extraordinary degree." They called him "that Francis," and Jean they called "Aunt Jean," in the old-fashioned way. The Harpers called themselves Crackers.

Among their closest friends were the Chesser family of Chesser's Island. From the women Jean learned how to cook an Okefinokee dinner of rice, stewed pork, dumplings, gravy, peas, rutabaga greens, hot biscuits, black grape jelly, and coffee, all unforgettably delicious. Two of the Chesser women took her by flat-bottomed boat, poled through the creeks to an island where huckleberries grew thick, ready to be made into jams and pies. Bear meat, too, was excellent and meant that one less bear would attack the family's razor-back hogs. After dinner there would be music, the songs accompanied on a homemade banjo. Jean did some research on her own and wrote an article, "Collecting Folk-Songs in Okefinokee Swamp," which was published in the *Vassar Quarterly*.

In 1933, when the Harpers returned to Swarthmore on a new grant that Francis had just received, they heard shocking news that the government was planning to put a ship canal through the Okefinokee Swamp. The Crackers were barely aware of the threat, and in any case were helpless. They had no conception of the size and power of the United States government, no notion of how it operated. The Harpers did know, and they were angry. It just so happened that Jean knew the man at the top, the president of the United States. On November 25, 1933, she wrote to him:

Dear Mr. Roosevelt:

There is a matter that needs your immediate attention— the preservation of the Okefinokee Swamp. Perhaps you re-call that a few years ago, Francis sent you some of his reprints on the Swamp. . . . For twenty odd years the naturalists and nature-lovers have been working for the preservation of this marvelous wilderness; unique in its nature not only in this country, but in the world. The character of its fauna, its flora, and its human life is unsurpassed. Two years ago the Senate Committee on Wild Life Resources visited the Okefinokee and submitted a report . . . recommending its purchase as a national wild-life refuge. But because of the depression noth-ing further has been done. We now learn of the project to put a ship canal through the swamp. You well know what this would mean to the beauty of the area and to the wild life. The destruction that would thus be brought on is unthinka-ble. Our hope lies in you, to stop the project before it goes farther, and spend the money in the purchase of the swamp for a reservation, where beauty and scientific interest may be preserved for all time. . . .

Jean also wrote at once to Anna Roosevelt, now Mrs. Curtis Dall, who answered promptly: "Dear Jean: I will most certainly take up the question of the proposed ship canal through the Okefinokee Swamp immediately with Father. It does seem a crime that such a thing should even be considered. . . ." On December 19, probably after promptings from his wife and daughter, the president answered: "Dear Jean: I too should hate to see the Okefinokee Swamp destroyed. Strictly between ourselves, I think there is much more chance of a ship canal going the southern way [through Florida] than through Georgia. I hope all goes well with you and the family. Very sincerely yours, Franklin D. Roosevelt."

Governmental projects were endlessly delayed or forgotten. No ship canal was built "the southern way" or through the Okefinokee, but two years later, in 1935, Jean had to write again from Swarthmore after a visit to the swamp. "My dear Mr. Roosevelt: My 'beloved Okefinokee' is still in danger, and again I want to ask your help. Every day's delay means more lumbering carried on and more of the swamp lost forever in its primeval state. It is a wilderness unique in its beauty and unsurpassed as a refuge for vanishing forms of wild life. The Biological Survey has investigated the area and favors its purchase by the Government. If you would but 'say the word' to bring this about, it would mean a permanent and priceless gain to the country. . . ." The president was making regular trips to Warm Springs, Georgia, for physical therapy. Jean suggested that on one of these trips he might come to see for himself "why the few of us who know and love the swamp become so 'impassioned' when we watch its gradual but steady destruction and see help within reach. . . ."

Roosevelt by this time was deeply involved in trying to control the vast and intricate bureaucracy that he had set up. He was facing bitter criticism from opponents in both parties who considered him "a traitor to his class" and could barely speak his name without sputtering about "that man in the White House," but he found time within ten days to respond. "February 18, 1935. Dear Jean: The enclosed comes from Mr. Darling [Chief of the Bureau of Biological Survey]. I would be entirely willing to have it [the Okefinokee Swamp] made a national monument but this would have to come through Congressional action. I am asking Mr. Darling to speak to the delegations concerned. Always sincerely, Franklin D. Roosevelt." The enclosed letter from Mr. Darling told the president that the swamp should indeed be a national monument and that a public road across the swamp, now being surveyed by the state of Georgia, could be stopped if the federal government would appropriate a million dollars to buy the area. Mr. Darling could discover no such funds. Roosevelt suggested that Mr. Darling might "try to get some Congressmen interested in the idea of a national monument." Time passed. Finally, two years later, through Roosevelt's continuing interest, by presidential proclamation the Okefinokee Swamp was made a wildlife refuge. Roosevelt's campaign song, "Happy Days Are Here Again," expressed the Harpers' feelings. Their fourth child, David Bartram, was about to be born, and the long struggle for the survival of the swamp seemed over.

It was not so. On May 26, 1937, Jean wrote to the president that the Biological Survey evidently knew nothing about how to maintain a natural wilderness. After the survey's technical director had assured Francis that "no planting of anything not native to the region is planned," the Harpers had just learned that 114 Asiatic chestnuts had been planted on Floyd's Island, supposedly to replace native chestnuts that had died in a blight. The normally calm and sunny-tempered Jean told the president that the bungling of his Biological Survey was "nothing short of a biological crime." Furthermore, the survey "in its anxiety to cater to the politically powerful duck-hunters" was planning to introduce non-native plants as duck food, when there was already enough duck food. And worst of all, "the CCC, with its record of devastation in other wilderness areas . . . had been turned loose on the Okefinokee, too," contrary to announced plans. Couldn't the president do something? "Always sincerely, Jean Sherwood Harper."

Roosevelt was in the midst of trying to reorganize the Supreme Court, but he looked into the Okefinokee matter at once, and found that Jean was correct. What was more, as he wrote to Henry Wallace, Secretary of Agriculture, on June 2, 1937, ". . . some kind of Japanese squirrel have been turned loose, apparently to go with the Japanese chestnuts. Please let me have a definite report on these rumors. If they are true, the chestnuts should be removed, the squirrels should be shot, and the duck feed eliminated. Why, oh why, can't we let original nature remain original nature? F.D.R." Henry Wallace replied, explaining, denying, promising to maintain the Okefinokee "as an inviolate wilderness area."

Yet a year later, Jean had to write again, this time to Eleanor Roosevelt. By 1938 the stormclouds of a great international war were gathering. "We don't want to bother the President at a time like the present," she wrote, "but something simply must be done at once, to stop the Biological Survey in its insane destructiveness." The latest project was to cut down all the big pine trees on Chesser's Island, one of the few islands still untouched by loggers. The Harpers themselves, with a gift of three hundred dollars from Aunt Margaret Sherwood, had now bought fifteen acres there and could not see the lovely pines cut down all around their tract without a protest. "Furthermore," Jean wrote, "we hear that the Government plans to build a paved highway right across Chesser's Island to its western edge. . . . It looks like just another case of giving the CCC something to do, no matter how much destruction it involves. . . . May I implore you to do whatever you can? . . ."

Mrs. Roosevelt could do something. A week later the president wrote to Henry Wallace: "I am told that the Biological Survey is 'at it again' in Okefinokee Swamp—and that this time they are about to cut down the big pine trees on Chesser's Island. . . . I do not want any trees cut down *anywhere* in the Swamp. F.D.R." Constant vigilance is the price of wildlife refuges.

The Harpers continued to spend most of every year at Swarthmore. In August 1940, when Germany launched heavy air assaults over Britain to prepare for an invasion of England, London was bombed nightly and even in small villages English people feared for their children. In America organizations were set up to "adopt" English children into American families for the duration of the war, or as long as necessary. Jennifer and Robin Colquhoun (a name well known in England, pronounced Kohoon) came to live with the Harpers at Swarthmore, where Francis was then working with the William Bartram Association on a book about the famous naturalist. The father of the English children was himself an amateur naturalist who was on military duty in London when he wrote to Francis on August 11, 1940: "One knew, of course, from the papers, that Americans were making these generous offers, but when it touches one person-

Jean Sherwood Harper with her four children and the Colquhouns

ally the contrast with these very grim days is so violent as to
make it difficult to write clearly. . . . So much that we value
has fallen of late years and days that I cannot express how
stimulating it is to feel this sympathy kindling on the other
side of the Atlantic."

The Colquhoun children had been brought up to live simply, and they fitted well into the Harpers' family life. Jean
treated them like her own children. Her older son, Robin,
has told what that meant. She was always supportive and was
so confident of her children's goodness that they tried to become what she believed. In this, Robin says, she was like
her mother, Mary Sherwood, whose "warm, inviting voice
was like enveloping arms." Jean was not a gifted hostess like
her mother—entertaining was an effort for her—but it came
naturally to add two English children to her own four; she

said that she had always wanted to have six children. The English parents sent financial support by one means or another, and the Harpers shared all they had. There were trips to Cornwall. Molly Harper remembers those days, which were part of the memories carried back to England when the Colquhouns returned: the cookie jar that was always full, the cold glasses of water drawn from deep down in the well on a hot summer day, the meals eaten on the screened back porch within view of Storm King Mountain, the trips down the winding path through the fields to the little brook for picnics and play. On their return to England in 1944, Jennifer at once joined a group of girls who were working on farms as Jean had done a generation earlier in the First World War.

In that summer of 1944 an Allied victory was within sight. While Allied forces were racing to the Rhine and Russian armies were sweeping westward, Jean Harper once more jogged the president's memory about the Okefinokee; she and Francis had heard rumors that the government might grant oil leases there. This time the answer took three weeks in coming and was drafted by the Department of the Interior rather than by Roosevelt himself, but it still began with the familiar, friendly "My dear Jean" and the message was reassuring; no oil drilling would be allowed. After many battles, the Okefinokee Swamp war was won at last. It can fairly be said that Jean's faithful concern came initially through her husband's love for the great swamp, but without her the cause would almost certainly have been lost. And it was she who gathered together Francis's voluminous records and papers—mountains of them—and organized them after his death so that an excellent book, *Okefinokee Album,* could be put together by Delma E. Presley and published by the University of Georgia. Without Jean there would have been no book. As for the swamp, *Okefinokee Album* assures us that "today the Okefinokee appears much as it must have to William Bartram two centuries ago when he described it as 'a most blissful spot of the earth' or to Francis Harper seven decades ago when he first journeyed to its heart. The piney woods, the swampy woods, and the waterways change but they endure."

Ironically, when the swamp became a refuge for its wildlife, it was no longer a refuge for humans. Bears could now safely attack hogs and cattle, wildcats killed young pigs, while Crackers who shot the "varmints" might go to jail. Gradually the Crackers moved away and found new homes, more comfortable but less free, outside the swamp. A few homesteads, on Cowhouse Island and Chesser's Island, were restored as exhibits, where tourists could see how the swamp people once lived. Thousands of visitors come each year to the Chesser homestead, probably unaware that it expresses the spirit of Jean Sherwood Harper. The theme of the exhibit is self-reliance, the title of the famous essay by Ralph Waldo Emerson, who called himself "more of a Quaker than anything else." He believed, as Quakerism taught, that God was a spirit present in all creation. In mankind, God was present as conscience, "a still small voice" that Quakers call the Inner Light. Therefore, when any conscientious person relied on the guidance of that Inner Light, self-reliance was reliance on God. This was Jean's faith.

It takes a special grace to live the life she lived for so many years, committing herself deeply to causes important to Quakers. She became the national secretary for the Women's International League for Peace and Freedom; she took part in peace vigils and peace marches. Yet her letters show that no cause ever outweighed her devotion to her family. The Harper children testify that Jean influenced them profoundly.

Golda Brown, Jean's lifelong friend and childhood tutor,

was one of the first Quakers she ever knew; Golda's daughter once summed up the meaning of Quaker life. She was about to be married to a man who could offer her no financial security, and her mother was concerned about the future. "But, Mother," said this young Quaker, "thee has made poverty so attractive." The same could be said of Jean.

Jean wrote her "I Personally" essay for the *Atlantic Monthly* in 1948. At the time, Francis had returned from a long and dangerous biological survey trip to Nueltin Lake in subarctic Canada, and the Harpers were spending the winter in an old stone barn near Cornwall, a building used in the summers for projects of the American Friends' Service Committee. "Barn-keeping is very different from house-keeping," Jean wrote. "Century-old stones and rafters constantly sift a fine dust over everything below. Crumbles of old plaster and cement and flakes of whitewash are frequent comrades. I have learned to live with it comfortably. It doesn't bother me and I don't bother it. . . . Luckily we have quantities of hot water, so we can wash clothes daily if we want to. I bake bread twice a week. . . . Our household goods are stored in *six* different garages in *three* different towns!

"So we turn the pages of our Book of Life and read on, fascinated. Will the next chapter bring us our longed-for and intensively searched-for home? Or will we wander on through the maze of years homeless, but secure? We are fast developing an inner security with a foundation rock that nothing can shake. Having no hearthstone of our own has not deprived us of a home formed from the ever-deepening bond between us . . . which even a world cataclysm cannot destroy." Jean and Francis were in love as long as he lived.

As it turned out, their four handsome children were to be the only grandchildren of Mary and Sidney Sherwood.

PENELOPE

Mary Sherwood wanted to have a son, who would of course be named for his adored father, Sidney. Still, when her first child, Gretchen, was born, she rejoiced that she had a daughter. Then came the second girl, Helen, who seemed to think that she should have been a boy. When Helen was a year and a half old, Mary did have a son, who lived only a few days. Jean was the third girl. During a family visit to Cornwall in 1898, the fourth girl, Penelope, was born. Her grandfather, old Dr. Beattie, wakened at midnight to hear the news of the baby's arrival, said, "What! Another girl? Oh, bosh!" and went back to sleep. Little Jean almost cried when her father carried her in to see the new baby in her mother's bed. "More baby?" she wailed. "Take she and frow she away in de dirt." Later, everyone in the family thought the story of Penelope's birth was a funny one, with the possible exception of Penelope herself.

She may have been named for the faithful, clever wife of Odysseus, but she must have known that her parents had hoped for a boy. In any case, as a child she wanted to be a carpenter. When she was two years old, there were carpenters at work all summer on the old family property. Uncle Matt was having the barn torn down and replaced by a house where he and his wife could come for vacations. At the same time, Mary and Sidney were building the big porch with its upstairs balcony at 51 Angola Road. Penelope, nicknamed Penny, followed the workers everywhere and made a special friend of one quiet old carpenter, saying over and over, "How do, man?" to hear his patient answer, "How do, baby?" The family thought that this was the start of Penny's love of carpentry, which was apparent from the first time she picked up a tool. She was to be Uncle Matt's most enthusiastic helper when he let the children handle saws, chisels, and hammers in building the log cabin. And Penny instinctively knew that people as well as things sometimes needed to be put together again. More than any of the other children, she considered Mary to be her special responsibility. Later, she extended the same concern to anyone who needed help.

Mary's stories about doctors made a deep impression on Penny, especially those about Grandpa Beattie's trips, on horseback or in two-wheeled carriage or sleigh, as "the doctor of the poor" who never refused to answer a call from the neediest cabins in the hills. Mary gave a vivid picture of her father in his heavy coat with cape and high fur collar, his fur cap, and mittens that kept him from freezing in the icy winters when he drove about on his errands of mercy; the story of Mary's sleigh ride with her father to care for Ike O'Dell's broken leg was unforgettable.

Penny's Grandfather Beattie became her hero and ideal. From early childhood she wanted to be a doctor, "like Grandpa." Not a city doctor, a country doctor.

As soon as she could remain seated on a pony's back, Penny began to ride. She rode Gypsy, and Midget, and later, Jack, the horse who kicked, and big Dan. Penny rode beautifully, like her mother. Her idea of bliss was to be mounted on horseback, a knight in shining tinfoil armor with wooden sword, the youngest of the Sherwood knights, riding dauntless in tournaments across the field below the house on Angola Road. Of all the family, Penny was the one who loved the horses and ponies best. She loved the mornings when it was her turn to feed and groom them in the stable with Gretchen. Horses and ponies had a private understanding with the ones who cared for them and rode them; it was the same with dogs, and there was always a dog in the Sherwood house. But the animals belonged to the whole family. Penny wanted a horse and a dog of her own, pets who would understand her completely. She must have thought she remembered the birth of the new baby, Sidney, because her mother so often told the story: "When Penny came in to see the baby, she drew her hand over his head and said, 'Little soft fur.' She evidently thought she had a new little pet animal."

But Penny soon learned that the new arrival was not a kitten or puppy. It was a baby and it was a boy, the one Mary had wanted, named for his father in place of the other baby Sidney who had died. This baby cried all the time because his unhappy mother could not nurse him and no other kind of milk suited him. For months he had his mother's entire attention. She carried him for hours on end, walking back and forth on the back porch in the summer heat.

Then came the terrible discovery that the constant carrying had done more harm than good. The baby's frail spine had developed a curve. It was Uncle Matt who recommended that little Sidney should be taken to Dr. Abraham

Jacobi, the great German pediatrician in New York City who had established and headed the first children's clinic in the United States. Dr. Jacobi's treatment was correct, and the baby's spine grew straight. But what of babies who could not be taken to a first-class doctor in a big city? Penny stored away all of these facts and questions in her mind.

She was not yet five years old when Gretchen's sledding accident focused the attention of the whole family on the treatment of broken bones. The local doctor had been guilty of gross negligence in failing to set Gretchen's leg straight before putting it into a plaster cast. No specialist existed anywhere near Cornwall. It took Uncle Matt to get Gretchen into the hands of the famous New York surgeon Charles McBurney; Gretchen owed her ability to walk and skate, and later to climb and ski, to the skill of those hands. Penny determined that she would be not only "the doctor of the poor," like Grandpa, but a surgeon as good as Dr. McBurney.

However, Penny's humanitarian instincts did not make her a saintly child. Years later, she wrote a short story in which her five-year-old self came to a decision. That year, Penny was bad-tempered. In the story she called herself Joan, a five-year-old whose mother said: "Perhaps if you ask God to help you be good, Joan dear, you can get over your crossness sooner." The mother, like Mary, was not a pious person, but "she had taught her children a few simple prayers, and had told them her ideas on religion, which, though far from radical, were not strictly orthodox." That night, in the story, Joan prayed earnestly, asking God to help her get over her "cross, tied-up-in-knots feeling," and woke in the morning confident that God had answered her prayer. But the moment she ran into the bathroom, there was Johnny (her small brother Sidney in real life), "in the tub

Mary Sherwood and the children on the steps of the log cabin

with *her* own pet pink soap. All her happy feelings disappeared, and she flew wrathfully at him to rescue her beloved sweet-smelling cake of soap. . . . There was no miraculous change in her outlook on life, as she had expected. God had failed her. No, she would never ask Him for another thing. If He wouldn't help her be good, which was what she had thought He wanted, she'd never pray again. Whatever she would get from life would be through her own efforts and mistakes, and God would get neither praise nor blame from her. All this of course did not formulate itself in her mind at once, but the foundation of it was laid that bright summer day, and it grew as Joan grew." No doubt Penelope saw the humor of this childish incident, as she remembered it, but it was a true report of her point of view from childhood onward.

Someone, probably Uncle Matt, took a picture of Mary

and the five children sitting on the steps of the log cabin after it was finished. Penny is covering her face as if she was not in the mood to have her picture taken, or as if the light hurt her eyes. Before long, she had to wear glasses. Behind the round, dark-rimmed spectacles, with her light hair parted down the middle and pulled straight back to be out of her way, she was plain, but she may have been too busy to care. When Gretchen's college friend, Prudence Ellis, came to visit at Thanksgiving, she wrote home: "Penelope is round and sturdy . . . bossy and vigorous. . . ." Like mother, like daughter.

Penelope was probably the most capable of all Mary's children. The year the ceiling fell in the big upstairs bedroom, Penelope was the best carpenter in nailing up the new panels between the exposed rafters. She was an expert by the summer when Uncle Matt supervised the building of the shack at Sagaponack, Long Island, and she seriously decided that if for any reason she could not be a doctor, she would be a carpenter.

Meanwhile, she was a success in all her studies, showing great powers of concentration, especially in science, and easily winning a scholarship to Vassar. She seems not to have made a happy start there. Jean was a sophomore and had many friends, but this was not of much help to Penny. Writing after college, she added an unfinished chapter to her story about herself. Now "Joan" was leaving home for Vassar: "Life was too exciting. Tomorrow she was to leave home for the first time, to go to college. What would it be like, being miles and miles away from home, from her family, in a crowd of strange girls? Would she like it? She wondered if morning would ever come, and then, while wondering, fell asleep." The scene changed to Joan's room at college. "Joan came into her room, slammed the door and threw herself on her couch. How she hated it all. How she longed for home! A month had passed. She had grown used to the strangeness. She rather liked her classes and some of her teachers. But all the time, something was pulling her. As long as she was working or playing, she could forget, but the minute she stopped, she would realize that her heart ached. Why was it that when you were a child and didn't appreciate it, you spent all your time at home, and as soon as you got older and knew how much you loved it, you had to spend most of your time away? It was all upside down and arranged wrong. Even the people you wanted to know didn't care anything about knowing you, and people you didn't care about were as friendly as anything. . . ."

In the last scene of this brief sketch, Joan sees a magnificent sunset from the window of her college room and feels that such beauty must have meaning. "Thunderstorms, wild driving rainstorms gave her the same feeling. Nothing calmed her stormy spirit as much as running out in a cold driving storm and fighting with the wind and rain for miles, careless of time or distance. 'I should have been a pioneer,' she often thought. 'It's fighting with the forces of nature that makes me feel life is worth living.'"

Yet this girl whose heart ached and who had a "stormy spirit" did make some college friends. There were other girls in her class who wanted to be doctors, though they were very few and felt like a breed apart. They knew that the road ahead would be rough, but the need was great. Their sense of mission deepened during their freshman year, in 1916, when an infantile paralysis epidemic frightened the whole country.

There were good times, too. Jean's friends were not Penny's friends, but it helped to have Jean herself in college for the first three years. And Sidney always came over the frozen river on his skates for the winter Ice Carnival. The objectionable baby who had infuriated her by using her pink soap was now preparing to go to Princeton. He was six feet tall and good-looking. It did not hurt to have an attractive brother. Penny's friends were glad to see a little more of him when she took them home for weekends of picnicking and riding on horseback along the trails in Black Rock Forest.

Aside from these interludes, few students were really carefree during Penny's college years. In the fall of 1916, the First World War was raging, and the outlook for the Allied forces was dark. Great offensives and counteroffensives brought enormous losses. By spring 1917, German submarine attacks on American shipping forced the United States into the war, and President Wilson's vision of a "war to make the world safe for democracy" stirred patriotic fervor. The sentiment for neutrality fled. At Vassar, "preparedness courses" were given, including "First Aid to the Injured," "Elementary Hygiene and Home Care of the Sick," and "Surgical Dressings." To conserve food there were weekly meatless days and wheatless days, and student farmers raised as much food as possible, so that the country at large would have more food to send abroad. Instead of spending money on luxuries, students raised a fund for war relief. They supported the American Ambulance Field Service in France.

Excitement ran high on campus. The atmosphere was tense. During the summer of 1918 came a critical German offensive, the second battle of the Marne, fought within striking distance of Paris, and at the same time the worldwide influenza epidemic was at its height. It was only later, long after the Allied victory and the armistice of November 1918, that the horror of the losses was known: ten million

Penny's graduation picture

killed in the war, twenty million wounded, and another ten million dead in the epidemic. It was a somber time to be a senior at college, about to face the world; for a girl determined to be a doctor it was a challenging time.

Penelope's graduation picture in June 1919 shows her looking straight ahead behind the round glasses, her curving lips firmly, purposefully set, facing the future as if with confidence. She had every right to feel confident; she had graduated with Phi Beta Kappa honors and had won a two-thousand-dollar scholarship to enter the Johns Hopkins Medical School. She had never wavered from the path she had long ago marked out for herself.

The influence of two men, her Grandfather Beattie and

her Uncle Matt, had been great. Even greater was the influence of her aunt, Dr. Mary Sherwood, the sister of Aunt Margaret Sherwood, whose career as a writer had haunted Gretchen. When Dr. Sherwood was born, Elizabeth Blackwell, the first woman doctor in the United States, had earned her degree at Geneva (now Hobart) College in upstate New York. She had founded the New York Infirmary for Women and Children that later included a women's college for the training of doctors, the first of its kind, though not on a par with the great American medical schools. The pioneer trail blazed by Elizabeth Blackwell had not been followed by the feet of many other women. When Penelope's Aunt Mary graduated from Vassar determined to study medicine at a first-class school, she had to go to the University of Zurich in Switzerland. No leading American medical schools accepted women students, and in any case, the great medical scientists of the day were all working in Europe or wanted to study there.

At school in Zurich, Aunt Mary had met another American medical student, Lilian Welsh, and together they took one of the first courses in bacteriology ever given anywhere. As a result, when the new Dr. Sherwood and Dr. Welsh returned to live in Baltimore, they became American pioneers in preventive medicine and public health, two specialties based on bacteriology. The Johns Hopkins Hospital had just opened, and a new medical school was being planned at the university. Mary Sherwood had such glowing recommendations from her professors in Zurich that she was offered what doctors called "the most coveted prize in Baltimore," a residency in the Johns Hopkins Hospital under the brilliant and influential Dr. William Osler. However, Mary's appointment depended on another woman accepting a residency also, in order to avoid unpleasantness for a single woman among so many men. Another woman doctor applied, but soon afterward she married, and neither she nor anyone else thought that marriage and a career in medicine could be combined. She withdrew, and as a result, the offer to Dr. Sherwood was withdrawn. Instead, she was taken onto the hospital staff as assistant to Dr. Howard Kelly, who was already famous for his work in gynecology and obstetrics.

By 1893, when the new medical school opened, women were admitted, and one of the early students under Dr. Kelly gave credit to Dr. Sherwood and Dr. Welsh for having paved the way by winning "the respect, admiration, and friendship of the distinguished medical school faculty. . . . Their presence in Baltimore had much weight in gaining the admission of women to the new medical school."

These two physicians at once became leaders in obstetrical services, infant care, preventive medicine in the public schools, and were among the founders of the American Child Health Association, which led to the establishment of the United States Children's Bureau. Dr. Sherwood was also ardent in the women's suffrage movement; she took care of Susan B. Anthony when that grand old pioneer became ill at a suffrage convention in Baltimore.

Penelope entered the Johns Hopkins Medical School with a ready-made reputation as Dr. Mary Sherwood's niece.

She seems not to have been daunted by her aunt's fame and thoroughly enjoyed the four years of grueling work. She had much in common with the other students. Like her, they were young, most of them were relatively poor, and they were serious about their work. They were very bright. Under a cool, enigmatic exterior they had the idealism and formed the warm personal relationships that would be part of a good doctor's personality. They were always short of sleep, and party-going was mostly confined to weekends, but joking and laughter went on every day. There were nine students from Vassar. Penny lived with two of them in an apartment near the medical school. Her 1921 Vassar reunion report read: "My present and future is pretty well assured, at least for the next three years. What will come after that, Heaven only knows. I'm living in an apartment with Edith Jackson, V. C. '16, and Helen Evarts, so you can imagine I have plenty of fun on the side."

But it was mostly work, and at Johns Hopkins the focus of Penelope's work was decided. One day another student asked the familiar question, "What will you do if you don't make it as a doctor?" She gave her usual answer: "I'll be a carpenter," and got the response, "If you like to work with chisels and hammers and saws, you'd better be an orthopedic surgeon."

The head of orthopedic surgery at Johns Hopkins was William S. Baer, a fine doctor, deeply committed to the Children's Hospital School, which he had helped to develop. He was at the height of his powers when Penelope became his student, and he directed her instinctive sympathy for suffering and her will to help especially toward children with weakened or deformed limbs and spines, children who had to be fitted with an artificial arm or leg, children in pain. Dr. Baer's students at Johns Hopkins were inspired by his vigor, his enthusiasm, and his example. They knew that during all of a summer as an assistant resident during his young days in a Boston hospital, he had worn a body cast so that he could know for himself how his patients felt. Penelope, assisting in operations with Dr. Baer, was not squeamish as women were expected to be. What troubled her was the sight of children on crutches or in wheelchairs. How did they feel?

She earned her M.D. degree in June 1923 and went at once to the Hospital for Women of Baltimore as an intern, waiting for a chance to begin specializing in orthopedic surgery. This chance came when she moved to a state institution for crippled children at Canton, Massachusetts, but it was a total disappointment. She wrote to Vassar classmates: "All I did was lose my good disposition (if I ever had one) at the disgraceful way things are done, or rather not done there." She left Canton in disgust.

Determined to cancel out that bad experience, she went for three months to New York City's Orthopedic Hospital, headed by Dr. Russell Hibbs. Again she was working with a pioneer. After diagnosis and treatment in the limited space of his city hospital, Dr. Hibbs sent his patients, mostly children, to a convalescent hospital that he had built at White Plains, New York. Here the children could stay for months, or even years, if necessary, in healthy outdoor surroundings, keeping up with their schooling and often learning a trade. Penelope was assigned to work at White Plains.

Many of the children were victims of infantile paralysis and tuberculosis of the spine for which the traditional treatment was to apply traction by the use of straps, buckles, and pulleys. The old method did little to relieve pain and seldom resulted in a cure; treatment went on for so many years that doctors sometimes lost interest in their patients. Dr. Hibbs had developed a new and radical technique of operation known as fusion, which was useful in many cases. His method was to put a patient under anesthesia and place the diseased or deformed limb or spine in proper position. He then made a plaster cast to hold the bones in place, and cut out the affected sections of bone through a hinged opening in the cast. Over a period of months, during which the patient had to be absolutely immobile, new bone formed, making a bridge to fill the gap. The new bone could not bend, but the patient was free of pain and could be active.

Dr. Hibbs's technique was so revolutionary that for years he was denied membership in the American Orthopedic Association, but his reputation grew with his many successes; 70 percent of his patients were completely cured. Dr. Hibbs had a great desire to pass on to his interns and residents his own idealistic attitude toward his calling as an orthopedic surgeon, and this must have appealed to Penelope. Helping the patient came first, without regard to self-glorification or financial reward. She applied for a residency at the New York Orthopedic Hospital and wanted it very much. Here was a place where she could be proud to work, continue to learn, and be able to go home to Cornwall for weekends. She met with a complete roadblock. The hospital had never accepted women as residents and did not want to begin now.

Instead, Penelope received a recommendation to the University of Iowa, where Dr. Arthur Steindler had opened a new children's hospital. He was willing to accept a highly qualified woman as a resident. Dr. Steindler was a Czechoslovakian. He had graduated from the University of Vienna and had become the colleague of all the leading pioneers in orthopedic surgery: Edward Albert, who was developing operations for bone fusion; Adolph Lorenz, internationally known for his treatment of children's problems, such as clubfoot, congenital dislocation of the hip, and curvature of the spine; Hugh Owen Thomas, famed for his skill in making "Thomas splints" and "Thomas surgical collars"; Sir Robert Jones, the British surgeon who had recently been knighted for his treatment of bones deformed by infantile paralysis. Arthur Steindler had also worked closely with the eminent American John Ridlon, who came from the New York Orthopedic Hospital and now headed the Home for Crippled Children in Chicago. All of these brilliant orthopedic surgeons on both sides of the Atlantic influenced each other and passed on to each other what they had learned. It was a true "laying on of hands."

In Iowa City, Dr. Penelope Sherwood received the benefit of this great heritage. Dr. Steindler stood beside his residents when they operated and made them review the results of each operation over a period of months. When there were failures, he suggested all the possible reasons. He cared deeply about his child patients, and he had a fatherly interest in the later careers of his residents.

Arthur Steindler loved Iowa City. Over the doorway of his big house on a bluff above the Iowa River was a Latin quotation: "More than all others, this corner of the earth smiles on me." But he would have understood why Penelope elected to leave Iowa City after two years of residency in his children's hospital to return to Cornwall. She had a smiling corner of the earth on another hill above another river, and it called her home to be a "doctor of the poor" in the small towns near Cornwall.

Ready at last to open her own office, she wrote in a 1926 bulletin to her Vassar classmates: "I am getting more thrilled with my work every day, except when I get frightened at the idea of getting out on my own feet, and having to operate without someone around to direct me." No one could be better prepared to face that challenge. Taught by Dr. Baer, Dr. Hibbs, and Dr. Steindler, she had had the best training that the United States could offer. Surely all would go well; she returned to Cornwall as one of the first women orthopedic surgeons in the United States.

Dr. Hibbs invited her to come down to the New York Orthopedic Hospital clinic twice a week to operate and to keep up with the latest advances in techniques. When she spoke of opening an office in Newburgh, he said that she would face difficulties; it would take time, patience, and persistence to start a private practice. But he saw the advantages of Newburgh. It was only ten miles from Cornwall and was much bigger. In any case, Dr. Hibbs said cheerfully, Newburgh could not be worse than any other place.

Penelope would of course have to buy a car; she could get a little British Morris for about two hundred fifty dollars. With three hundred dollars from Aunt Margaret to help cover her first expenses, she opened her office in 1928 at 202 Grand Street in Newburgh. Her mother sat at a desk in the waiting room, ready to answer calls and make appointments, saving the cost of a secretary. Few calls came, and even fewer appointments were made, "only about one a week," as Penelope afterward described those lean days.

Not one of Mary's children was in a position to help their mother. Sidney had just married and wanted to establish his new household. He had tried mining and ranching out West without success. Jean and Francis, camping in the Okefinokee Swamp, were barely solvent and had two children to care for. Both Gretchen and Helen were struggling to support themselves. Penelope, an orthopedic surgeon, with superb training and experience under distinguished teachers, was the only one with a chance to change the picture for everyone in her family. Yet, ten years after graduation from college, she was living at home, depending on her mother for room and board.

Then came the stock market crash of September 1929, bringing hard times for doctors as well as for businesses. Patients could not pay their bills, and many who needed medical care put off going to a doctor. Mary had been paying a small fee to play golf on the local course. That pleasure had to go. A month after the crash, perhaps writing beside Penelope's silent telephone, she began a diary:

OCTOBER 1, 1929. I am 65 years old and my life has been full, beautiful, and strenuous. Every great joy that I have known has passed; even the little pleasures have ended. Now I am giving up my last and best recreation—golf. Money is so scarce. I cannot pay my club dues—perhaps later I can take it up again, for I long to get out and away from daily routine or I shall be more unfit to be of any help to Penelope, who is making such a brave effort to get a start in her orthopedic surgery. So much is against her.

My children have good intelligent brains, well trained minds, and yet every one of them has to struggle harder than the majority for existence. What was my great mistake in their early training? too high ideals? Perhaps my not having ever earned my own daily bread, I did not realize what it meant to cope with the world. They should have learned a trade in this industrial age.

OCTOBER 2, 1929. Spent morning in Penelope's office writing letters. After lunch played golf, which as usual gave me a better vision, carrying me back to the days when my Sidney was beside me, teaching me by his wisdom and great love how to face life. I need golf, not so much the game itself, but its associations . . . those wonderful memories of our life together rush into my mind, making my heart strong to "sit up and face it." I prefer playing alone. But enough, my children must not know how childish I am acting. I shall ever have Sidney's great love for me as the cornerstone of my life. It is *firm*. *Nothing* can move it. I do not *need* these outward things to remind me of its power and beauty. Here I turn another page as I polish and set aside my clubs.

A future source of income for the Sherwood family went down the drain at this time: money, stocks, and bonds that Aunt Belle, the missionary, Aunt Margaret, and Dr. Mary had intended to leave to Mary Sherwood and her children.

Thousands of dollars dwindled to mere hundreds. Dr. Mary's estate suffered a disaster. She lost the savings of a lifetime, as Aunt Margaret explained in a letter during the Depression that followed the stock market crash: "Coal bonds, railroad shares declined, or went wholly to the bad." The Baltimore Trust Company that handled Dr. Mary's money went bankrupt.

Although Penelope had almost no patients who could pay their bills, she was soon very busy. At Newburgh, Haverstraw, and Poughkeepsie there were hospital clinics that offered free care to patients who could not pay. These clinics were manned by doctors of good reputation, working free of charge. Penelope was invited to serve and began treating patients all up and down the Hudson River valley. Through the clinics her own reputation grew, and other doctors referred patients to her for orthopedic treatment and operations that were beyond their own ability. She later said, "They handed me the wrecks."

Little by little, she built up her paying practice. Dr. Hibbs referred a patient to her, who said, "They told me you were the best orthopedic surgeon in Orange County." Penelope smiled inwardly. At the time, she was the *only* orthopedic surgeon in the county.

In the depths of the Depression, help came to Cornwall and to Penelope. In good times and bad, the town had always owed much to the Stillman family. It was the Stillmans who gave six hundred acres and a million dollars to make Black Rock Forest a reserve for research in forestry. It was the Stillmans who gave the property for the Storm King Golf Club, where Mary had been playing. And in 1931, Dr. Ernest Stillman built a sixty-five-bed hospital in Cornwall. Penelope was immediately asked to establish and to head an orthopedics department. The staff, ten men and one woman,

Penny with the medical staff of Cornwall Hospital

Penelope, had their picture taken as a group on the porch of the new hospital. She appeared, as friends and patients ever afterward remembered her, in command of the situation, whatever it might be, but gentle. The angry little girl of years ago had grown into a woman with angelic patience. She may have seemed somewhat mannish, this solitary woman working among men, like a twentieth-century Joan of Arc, but an article about her forty years later paid tribute: "Her brisk professional manner didn't obscure a great tenderness for the sufferings of mankind. . . . Her generosity to those who could not afford medical attention became a legend around town." Every family with children knew her, because she was appointed as physician for the Cornwall school system. She was following in Dr. Mary's footsteps and fast catching up.

After the opening of the Cornwall Hospital, Penelope

made a good living as a doctor. She installed a new oil-burning furnace to keep the old house on Angola Road really warm at last in the severe winters. No longer would Mary have to climb up and down the cellar stairs to shovel coal into the old furnace. There were gifts from Aunt Penny to Jean's children, who took the place of children of her own that she would never have. There were gifts and loans to everyone in the family, even before they could ask for help. If an operation was needed, Penny would find the best doctor and pay the bills. In later years, when Jean and Francis moved to Chapel Hill, North Carolina, Jean wrote: "Penny, you are wonderful to keep on taking care of us even at such a distance. Your offer to pay for a specialist for me is just like you, but I'm sure I don't need one. . . . The dress you got me, Penny, is a joy. I wear it a lot. Because it's a solid color I can wear different pins, or necklaces, or scarves, and that is fun. I get many compliments on it. I can't thank you enough for being so generous. . . ."

For herself Penelope did not want much, but she bought the well-cut suits that a successful woman doctor should wear—and for seventy-five dollars she bought a beautiful horse called Silver. All the other horses and ponies had died of old age or been sold, but she had dogs of her own, and with her horse and dogs she found that perfect understanding for which she had always longed. Still better, she found herself surrounded by more human love than she had ever expected. Babies all up and down the Hudson River valley were named for her. One Newburgh mother had a baby born with a dislocated hip. She could not have paid a bill, and Penelope did not send one. Nine weeks later she received pictures of the baby, Susan Penelope, one showing her peacefully asleep, the other happily smiling. The hip had been corrected and had healed perfectly. The mother wrote:

". . . I haven't had her to clinic as it's so cold and I've no way to get her there. I haven't had her out since Christmas day. It was 12° below zero here at 5:30 a.m. today. Am glad we have a good heating stove. Write, call or come to see us whenever you find time. . . ."

Penelope "found time" and never lost interest. One former patient, Fay Sennas, has given a detailed account of Penelope's long and devoted care of her in the Rehabilitation Hospital at Haverstraw. She remembered the bright blond hair and blue eyes of this doctor, the only woman on the staff, and she wrote what had happened. She was admitted to the hospital and was put into long plaster casts to straighten both legs, which were bent from sitting in a wheelchair for four years following poliomyelitis. "After 6–8 weeks, the casts were removed and . . . it was decided that I required numerous surgical procedures in order to enable me to wear braces. For the following year I underwent bilateral tibial osteotomies [cutting out sections of bone in the shins, as Dr. Hibbs might have done], bilateral hip flexion releases [to restore motion] and an opponens transplant on the left hand [an operation on bones and tendons]. Following removal of the last plaster cast, I underwent an intensive course of physical therapy and was measured for long leg braces fifteen months after having been admitted to the hospital. Dr. Sherwood guided me through all the various steps which finally progressed to being able to go home for the Christmas holidays with my new braces and crutches and take a few steps. Dr. Sherwood felt I had more than earned going home, since I had spent the previous Christmas in a plaster cast from my chest to my toes. She had the rare ability to put herself in the patient's position. . . ." Fay continued her schooling at the hospital until she graduated from the eighth grade, receiving her diploma from the hands of

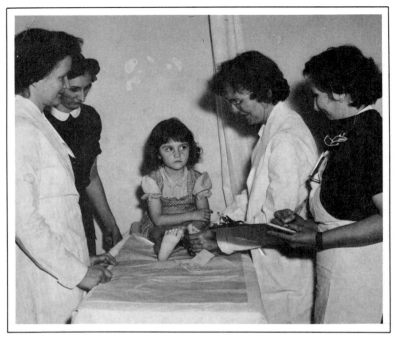

Penny treats a young patient

Helen Hayes, the famous actress, who had long served on the Board of Visitors. The hospital was later rebuilt and named in her honor, the Helen Hayes Hospital. Two months after graduation, Fay was able to go home and begin a useful life. She became secretary to the medical director at the hospital, attributing her success to Penelope Sherwood's care, which continued for eighteen years. Fay called her "a guardian angel . . . a rare and loving individual." No physician could ask for more. Few have given more.

When the United States entered World War II in 1941, there was an immediate demand for doctors to serve overseas, and Penelope became once more the only orthopedic surgeon in the area around Cornwall. "The staff at the [Helen Hayes] Rehabilitation Hospital used to tease me," she said later. "I drove the Storm King Highway through ice and snow. I didn't care about the weather." That road, curving in and out along the edge of the great mountain, high above the river gorge, also took her to West Point. The military academy was seriously understaffed during the war, and Penelope was called in as consultant on difficult cases. Once a month, or oftener in emergencies, she took care of young men who had broken an ankle or a rib, dislocated a knee, or suffered a concussion in sports. There were occasional automobile or truck accidents that might result in a broken pelvis or a fractured spine. Retirees and the families of married personnel were served, too, including newborn babies.

Just at this time, with the need for her services at its peak, Penelope's ability to work was threatened. Mary Sherwood, writing from Cornwall, mentioned it in a letter to Eleanor Roosevelt, who was now living in the White House but had never lost touch with her old friend: "Penelope is having a serious time with a bad infection in her right thumb. The surgeon hopes to save the joint. She is having every care in our Cornwall Hospital." Mrs. Roosevelt answered by return mail and sent flowers "to bring a little cheer" to Penelope. For a surgeon, no loss could be worse; Penelope's work depended on her hands. Though Mary did not say so, she must have relived the terrible days forty years before when her husband had died of an infection in his thumb. But there was a great difference now. Sir Alexander Fleming had discovered penicillin, the life-saving antibiotic, and by 1941 it was being used for war casualties. Civilian use was limited, but there may have been a supply at West Point. By whatever means, Penelope's hand was saved.

The love and admiration between Mary and Penelope grew with every passing year. Mary said that she had her

own personal physician. Now in her eighties, she still skated
on the pond, and Penelope knew that it kept her mother
young. She sent Sidney a snapshot of Mary on skates. When
he wrote back, "Penny, for heaven's sake, keep mother off
the ice," she answered, "Don't ever say that. If she snaps
her hip, we'll fix it."

Penny was working seven days a week, but she kept close
to all of her sisters and to Sidney. Jean recorded one family
reunion at Angola Road: "Never will we forget the vivid picture as we drove away from the old house this perfectly
beautiful morning—clear, brilliantly sunny, the mountains
and all vegetation a lush green. This greenness framed the
picture—the white house with dark green blinds, and just in
front, two beloved figures; Penny, tall, blond-haloed in her
green-blue plaid dress, her arm around Mamma's shoulders;
that familiar figure in blue, erect, firm-shouldered, smiling
and waving as we waved back from the car. High-hearted,
valiant as always!" Penny would have laughed at the idea of a
saintly halo and probably did not know that she had become
beautiful.

Early in the war years, she made a new friend. This was
Hazel Brill Jackson, an artist, who specialized in sculpturing
animals. She lived on a wooded hillside at the edge of Newburgh, in a studio converted from a barn behind the big
house owned by her family. The studio was filled with fine
furniture and works of art from European travels; Hazel had
been educated by governesses and in the best art schools in
Boston and Rome. She was herself a young woman of striking good looks, and she knew a beautiful sight when she saw
one. She first saw Penny from the back porch of the Sherwoods' house. Penny had been riding, mounted on Silver,
and now was galloping across the field below the house, her
honey-colored hair—so Hazel described it—lying loose on

Mary skating at the age of 84

her shoulders. As an artist, Hazel responded strongly to both horse and rider; this unknown woman with the trim figure was riding magnificently. She soon learned that Penny was in every way an admirable and lovable person. They became close friends.

With two other friends, a nurse and a gym teacher, Penny had a standing invitation to come to Hazel's studio at Upwey every Saturday night for supper. Sometimes Gretchen, Helen, or Jean came, when they happened to be home. Afterward they would talk, sitting around the fireplace, about life, their work, and their beliefs. They talked about animals, especially horses. Often, Spain was in their minds, and the aftermath of its recent savage Civil War. Gretchen spoke about the epic Spanish knight, El Cid, in her *Tale of the Warrior Lord*. Hazel made a sculpture of Don Quixote on horseback with Sancho Panza and his donkey. For a bronze *Crusader*, mounted and trampling a dragon, she won a prize from the American Academy of Design. This was the work of art that the Sherwood family gave to Vassar in memory of Gretchen.

More and more Hazel was attracted to the idea of a knight on horseback, and she connected this image with Penny. When Yale University Press asked Hazel to illustrate a collection of poems, *Castle in Spain*, she drew three pictures. One was a castle with battlements and turrets, standing on a rugged cliff, seen against a billowing white cloud. One was a patient donkey. The third was a knight with his sword raised to slay a dragon. One night, absorbed in her work, she dreamed that the knight entered the castle. She went in with him and saw words carved on a stone wall, "No high endeavor shall prove vain." She heard the words spoken. To Hazel, in some mysterious way, the words meant Penny, and she carved them above her own fireplace. She made a bust of Penny, young, strong, and beautiful as she had once been, with her hair curling against her shoulders.

The friends who met at Hazel's studio were welcome to try out their own talents in the room where easels, paints, modeling tools, and plaster casts were kept. Penny took up sculpture only as a hobby, but Hazel saw that she would have made a fine artist. Penny had an instinct, born of long years with carpentry and surgery, for the use of the tools and the making of plaster casts. She made an excellent marble copy of *Saint John the Baptist as a Boy* by the great Italian sculptor Donatello. Perhaps the emaciated body with the otherworldly face, pathetic in its intensity and vulnerability, reminded her of some young patient of her own. Yet Saint John was a curious choice, because when the friends at "Upwey" talked about religion, Penny always said, "I'm an atheist." "No!" they would protest. "You can't be—not you, Penny, of all people." But she insisted, adding, "I do believe in reincarnation." She never explained what she meant by this, but certainly Cornwall thought of her and her grandfather, old Dr. Beattie, the pioneer country doctor, as two of a kind.

Hazel's bust of Penny stands in a hall of the Cornwall Hospital, with a plaque below it:

PENELOPE SHERWOOD, M.D. 1898–1971
Pioneer Woman Orthopedic Surgeon 1928–1971
Established Orthopedic Department
in the Cornwall Hospital

✤ 6 ✤

SIDNEY—AND MARY AGAIN

W hen a boy is named for his father, the name can be a burden. If the father is not admirable, the boy carries a troublesome load. If the father is almost perfect, his son can try to be like him, or he can rebel. Sidney Sherwood, Jr., had a father who was perfect in the eyes of his wife and of the children who remembered him. Young Sidney did not remember him, but he knew that it was up to him to be another Sidney. If he was not, his mother would be deeply disappointed, and he must not disappoint her. He knew this as soon as he could understand anything.

His father had been so proud of him. Laughing and wondering if a father should kiss a boy, his last act before leaving Cornwall for the fatal trip to Ballston Spa was to kiss the month-old baby.

They never saw each other again. Then came the long hot summer after his father's death, when Mary fought for her baby's life and health, never counting the cost to herself. "I was unable to nurse him," she wrote later. "I tried different baby foods, but he was under-nourished, and cried a great deal. Trying to soothe him, I would carry him in my arms for hours, walking on the porch. I would hold his head on my left arm, leaving my right hand free to caress him. One morning while bathing him, I held him up under his arms and for the first time noticed that his legs curved to the left and his spine showed a decided lateral curve." Matt came that evening and was surprised and concerned about the baby. He made an appointment for Dr. Abraham Jacobi to examine Sidney in New York City, and the great pediatrician said, gruffly, "Who has been caring for this baby?" "I have," answered Mary, and described how she had spent months carrying Sidney. "You have done it," the doctor announced. The blame was hers. He told Mary to allow no one to fondle the baby. He must be kept on his back until he was ready to sit up of his own accord.

Under Dr. Jacobi's treatment, Sidney was able to enjoy the fun of his first Christmas at Cornwall, in spite of his bad back, and by the age of two he was walking. His back was perfectly straight, he weighed forty pounds and was a beautiful child, with big blue eyes, golden curls, and red cheeks. But the story of that first summer was often told, with its ironic mixture of sacrificing love and guilt, and it must have helped to seal the bond between mother and son. Sidney was the apple of his mother's eye. His sisters, who alternately petted and teased him, called him Sid. They pooled their saved-up pennies to buy him a big white wooly dog on wheels.

Mary saw to it that he was included in whatever the girls were doing, if it could possibly be arranged. He was too young to go to dancing school with them, but he went to the final costume party. Dressed as a dragon, he crawled around the edge of the dance hall, watching for a chance to switch

Four-year-old Sidney with his mother and sisters

his dusty tail against the white stockings of a little girl who had once teased him. He soon learned that girls could fight as well as tease. He would not forget Penny's rage when he played with her pink soap in the tub.

All of his sisters were bigger and stronger than he was, and in spite of his healthy looks and red cheeks, Sid had weak lungs. During a severe winter when he was three years old, he had pneumonia, which at that time, before penicillin and sulpha drugs, was a deadly disease for the very young as well as the very old. For two weeks Sidney was dangerously ill. "It was bitterly cold," Mary wrote, "the temperature being below zero much of the time. I tried to keep the coal furnace at an even temperature of 70 degrees, night and day. Sidney needed attention at least every two hours." When the anxious weeks ended and he began to improve, Mary was exhausted. A local doctor gave her a tonic mixed with some cocaine to keep her from collapsing. She vividly remembered the effect—"exhilaration and loss of all responsibility." Matt heard of this before the cocaine could do lasting damage, and prescribed a harmless tonic in its place.

Everyone knew that Sid was Mary's favorite child. She never meant to show special love for him, but she could not help cherishing him the most because he had given her the most pain and anxiety. Still, she wanted him to be manly, not spoiled, and even as a small boy, he did his part of the family chores. When Mary shook down cinders from the furnace, Sid hitched Gypsy to a little sledge and hauled them from the cellar door to dump them on the driveway. As soon

Sidney with his sisters and the horses

as he was old enough, he worked on nearby farms in the summer and earned money to buy a calf. The calf became a cow and produced another calf, and milk. Sid sold the calf and learned to milk, selling all the milk the family could not drink, and saving every penny for college. He would, of course, be going to Princeton, like his father.

Mary was trying to teach her children courtesy, honesty, the importance of hard work, unselfishness, and the joy of loving and serving others. But she now thought that perhaps there was still something missing. This came about after Gretchen said one day, "When we lived in Baltimore I always knew when it was Sunday because we always had waffles, but now I don't know when it's Sunday anymore." Sunday should not be a question of waffles or no waffles. Mary rented a pew in the Episcopal church at Cornwall.

As a result, by the time Sid was ten, the rector was urging him to join the boys' choir in the Episcopal church. Sid could not sing, but he was a good-looking addition to the procession. All went well until one Sunday when he heard the rector and the choirmaster having an argument, almost a fight. Sid was disgusted, and besides, as he told his mother, he wanted to say prayers in his own way, not to read them out of a book. She told him that in that case he might try the Quaker meeting, where he could say his own prayers. The next Sunday he went off by himself from Angola Road, through Cedar Lane to the Quaker meetinghouse, and there he attended regularly for several years, until the entry of the United States into the First World War forced him to make a critical decision.

Meanwhile, his sisters, one by one, were going off to Vassar and bringing home their friends for the famous Cornwall weekends. Sidney was too young to be part of their fun and games and did not much appreciate their teasing and kissing of the "little brother." But he did not mind being pressed into service for driving the wagon, loaded with giggling girls, to and from the railroad station, and he cheerfully made himself useful with saddling horses and building campfires.

One year when he was still in elementary school, the house needed to be painted, a job that would cost more than two hundred dollars if a man were hired to do it. Jean and Penny, who were in high school, insisted that they could do the painting themselves and save the two hundred dollars. In old bloomers and middy blouses they set to work, managing the ladders with Mary's help, while Sid, not to be left out, climbed to the top of the longest ladder and reached all the highest spots.

His winter Fridays were busy. In the morning Mary made dozens of sweet, crusty crullers. In the afternoon a French teacher came by train from Newburgh to give a lesson in French conversation to the Sherwood children who still had to pass college examinations in a foreign language. Sid was not too young to start; Mary and eight of her friends were not too old. After crullers and coffee, Sid would take Mademoiselle to her train and get ready for his Friday evening dancing class. This was his own idea. He asked twelve of his classmates to join, each paying thirty-five cents to a high school boy who was an excellent dancer and could teach them how to waltz and fox-trot. After supper the class arrived and rolled up the rugs in the hall, the library, and the living room, where Mary waxed the floors once a month. Most of the furniture was moved to the back porch. A wind-up Victrola provided the music, such as "The Blue Danube Waltz," songs from *The Merry Widow*, "Alexander's Ragtime Band," and "Oh, You Beautiful Doll." It was wonderful fun. At the end of the evening came more crullers and hot cocoa before the dancers went off into the frosty night and the Sherwoods put their house together again.

Sid had never thought of going to college anywhere except

Princeton, but this might be no simple matter. His sisters had needed tutoring in order to meet the Vassar requirements when they entered from Cornwall High School. Sid was not an outstanding student, and Mary decided that he, too, needed extra help. In the fall of 1917 he entered the Storm King School to prepare for Princeton. He had always been taught by women and lived in a woman's world at home. Storm King would be different and harder. The teachers were men and the courses were geared for students who had to pass college entrance exams. Even getting to school was harder. He had earned enough to buy a little Morgan riding horse for fifty dollars. On every school day during his two years at Storm King, he fed, groomed, and saddled Barton, cleaned the stable, took a bath, and dressed before eating breakfast. By seven-thirty he was galloping across the field to the brook road and three miles up Deer Hill to reach school by eight o'clock. His classmates at Storm King called him "Paul Revere." How Mary paid the tuition fee is not known. Aunts and uncles may have helped, and Sid certainly did his part in covering his expenses.

Another responsibility had to be faced that year. In 1918 the armed forces were asking for volunteers and a draft had been imposed. Sid wanted to enlist in the army; at the same time, three of his friends joined the Quaker Meeting to avoid the draft. Sid settled the dilemma by resigning from the Meeting, though in the long run he did not enlist. Perhaps the medical examining board turned him down for some reason, or someone may have persuaded him that the only son of a widowed mother should not volunteer. In any case, by the time Sid entered Princeton in September 1919, the war was over, the controversial Treaty of Versailles had been signed, and it remained for Sid's generation to pick up the pieces and try to put the world together again.

The Princeton of 1919 was different from the college that Sid's father had known. The town was bigger and the campus had grown. New college buildings of gray stone in "collegiate Gothic" style were handsomely set in tree-shaded lawns. In an earlier day, most of the students had been Presbyterians, many of them in training for the ministry. In Sid's class, only thirteen planned to become ministers, and there were students of all faiths, interested in a wide variety of careers. On Prospect Street there were now eating clubs, the social centers of the college, to which two-thirds of the upperclassmen, juniors and seniors, belonged. These clubs had barely existed when Sid's father had gone to Princeton, and he had not belonged to one. Woodrow Wilson, as president of Princeton, had tried to do away with them, calling the lot of nonmembers "a little less than deplorable." But the clubs survived because the students wanted them, and when Sid Sherwood came to Princeton, he realized what membership in a club would mean: It would cost time and money, and he had little to spare; but not to belong would be grim. To be "in," or not "in." Before the war, it was almost all that mattered.

After World War I more students were serious, and during Sid's first years at Princeton the Twenties had not yet begun to roar. The Volstead Act had been passed in 1919, over President Wilson's veto from the White House, bringing in the era of prohibition. This had been the hope of the nineteenth-century temperance movements; the twentieth century was about to try it out as the law of the land. Enforcement soon proved to be impossible. On college campuses there were nondrinkers as well as drinkers, but illegal drinking, smuggling, and bootlegging were widespread. Some students went on drinking binges that lasted for weeks. Four to one, students in Sid's class were opposed to

The family gathered for a photograph about the time Sidney was in college

prohibition and thought that drinking was not morally wrong.

Some thought that even dancing and card playing were morally wrong. Sid enjoyed both, but it is a fair guess that he did not drink or spend much time playing cards or dancing; he was too busy, and he could not afford to waste a cent. There were three ways in which a student could earn his way through Princeton. He could win a scholarship, if his grades were high; he could get a student loan from the college; or he could have a job on campus. As the only son in a family of scholarship winners and Phi Beta Kappa graduates, Sid was irked by the fact that his grades were not high enough for him to win a scholarship, and he had no prospects of paying off a loan. He got a job waiting on tables in the Commons dining halls.

He was also enjoying the many activities at Princeton that cost little or no money. He joined the freshman cross-country squad, the crew squad, the debating team of the Whig Society—one of Princeton's literary clubs—and became vice-president of the Woodrow Wilson Club. To keep him even busier, by his sophomore year he was made manager of the entire waiters' corps. He was not altogether happy with being a waiter, but students working on campus jobs were never thought of as "outsiders." They had as good a chance as anyone else to be elected to a club at the end of the sophomore year. At the end of that year, with twenty-two other classmates, Sid was invited to join the Gateway Club, which attracted some "brains" but was not sought after by the "big wheels."

In 1920, Jean Sherwood was tutoring Anna and Elliott Roosevelt at Hyde Park. She brought them home to Cornwall several times, and it was probably then, on some weekends home from Princeton, that Sid met Anna. She was only fourteen but already more sophisticated socially than Sid was at nineteen, and she had suffered emotional wounds that he had never felt. She was consciously torn with conflicting feelings about her parents. There was something wrong between them and between her mother and Granny Roosevelt. She did not understand their troubles, but often she had a guilty desire to get away from all of them. She liked the life the Sherwoods lived at Cornwall, and she liked Sidney. They did not lose touch during his junior and senior years, and he was falling in love with her. She knew it. But he was not her only beau. One of the others was Curtis Dall.

Curtis was a member of the class of 1920. If he had graduated he would have been one of those men voted by his classmates as "best looking," "greatest social light," "most thorough gentleman." At parties he was always the center of a group that gathered around the piano. He played well and had a lusty singing voice. At Princeton he had been in the glee club and the choir. He had tried out for the track and crew teams but had really shone at tennis. He was on the freshman prom committee. He was a member of Whig Hall and belonged to the prestigious Cap and Gown Club, listing himself as an Episcopalian and a Republican. But the 1920 *Nassau Herald* noted under his handsome picture that "Dall left Princeton, March 1, 1918, and enlisted in Naval Aviation. Ensign, A.E.F. [the American Expeditionary Force]. He did not return to college." Shortly after his return from military duty, Curt began to work on Wall Street. His name reappeared on lists for debutante parties; he was one of New York's most eligible bachelors.

Anna may have been aware of how much Granny Roosevelt controlled the lives of her son, his wife, and all their children. She controlled them through her money. Franklin Roosevelt's jobs carried great prestige, but the salaries were never large enough to cover the expenses of a house or an apartment in New York City, the house at Campobello, the steady stream of servants involved in this way of life, the school bills for five children, and large costs in traveling and political campaigning. Franklin and Eleanor Roosevelt were often short of money, and Granny helped to fill those gaps in a major way. Like the rest of her family, Anna always felt under great pressure to please Granny by taking her advice.

Anna was attending Miss Chapin's School for Girls in New York City, an excellent place as preparation for college or as a "finishing school." She did not fit in well at Miss Chapin's and thought that no one wanted to be her friend, but she put up with it because she had no choice and because for her it was a "finishing school." There would be no college for Anna. Granny bluntly said that girls who went to college only learned how to act like old-maid "bluestockings" whom no attractive man would want to marry. After Miss Chapin's, according to Granny's plan, Anna would come out at Newport and have a winter abroad. She would then marry the most eligible bachelor available and live happily ever after. Her father and mother agreed but thought that she had better have some sort of training so that she could earn her own living if necessary. They suggested a short course or two in agriculture at Cornell, which could be arranged later, after Anna returned from Europe. She might study fruit farming and come home to manage the Hyde Park orchards, the job that her father had once offered to Jean Sherwood.

By the time Anna reached her eighteenth birthday, she had known Sidney for four years and often went to see him at Cornwall. Snapshots were taken on hikes and picnics in the mountains, Anna young and lovely, sitting with Mary Sherwood or with Jean; Sidney, tall, handsome, and smiling, wearing a khaki shirt, jodhpurs, and riding boots, a happy young man. He knew that there could be no formal engagement to Anna until he had an established position and could offer her a home, but the Sherwood family, seeing Sid and Anna together, believed that she cared for him and would marry him when he had earned the right to ask her father for her hand. If Sid and Anna talked about fruit farming, that was only wishful thinking for some vague, rosy future. Realistically, Sid's major field at Princeton was political science and economics, following in his father's footsteps, and he planned eventually to go on for graduate studies. At graduation the *Nassau Herald* of 1923 included the information that Sidney Sherwood, "Sid," was an Episcopalian and a Democrat intending "to study economics at Harvard or Columbia, and then engage in foreign exchange banking." In the meantime he had a letter of recommendation from an old friend of

Sidney in the doorway of a mountain cabin with his mother, Penelope, and Jean. Anna Roosevelt is in the foreground.

his father that had resulted in the offer of a job starting immediately after graduation, in the credit department of the prestigious Bankers Trust Company on Wall Street. He accepted it.

Whatever Sid and Anna may have planned for the future, Granny Roosevelt had planned Anna's life for the present—first the debut in August at Newport, then the winter abroad, for all of which she herself would pay the bills. If she knew anything about Sid, she must have thought that Anna could do much better. Other young men, too, were in love with Anna, and she was writing to all of them. Eleanor Roosevelt talked to Anna about Sid. She did not oppose him as a prospective husband for Anna—she liked him very much—but with his future still uncertain, she did not want the romance to move too fast. On the whole, she agreed with Granny that coming out at Newport and taking the grand tour of Europe were a good idea. To fill July, she arranged for Anna to have a riding and camping vacation in the

Arizona desert with the Greenway family, friends who had mining interests in Bisbee, near the Mexican border. They had a daughter about Anna's age.

From Arizona, Anna wrote cheerfully to her mother, describing a trip 2,200 feet underground to see a copper mine, "a little scary, but good fun." She had enjoyed some long horseback rides and had slept one night in the open. "I love it out here," she wrote. "The people are so hospitable and friendly, and everything is so 'big.' The thought of Newport is more unattractive than ever. . . . Gee! I wish Newport would blow up and bust."

But when August came, Newport had not blown up and busted. Years later, Anna remembered the conflict with Granny, who was backed up by Anna's mother: "I was informed that I had to come out in society, and I died. And I *wasn't* going to come out. And Granny said, 'You *are*.' And I went to mother and she said, 'Yes, you must.'" Anna's father would take no part in the controversy.

So Anna faced Tennis Week at Newport, wearing the new clothes that Granny had bought for her. After Newport, Anna had more beaus than ever. Sidney must have known that he had stiff competition. But it was at Newport that a gossipy and heartless cousin told Anna about her father's romance that had nearly wrecked her parents' marriage years before. Now she knew what was wrong between them and saw that life in the Roosevelt family was much more complicated than she had ever guessed. She wanted to cut loose and get away as soon as possible.

That fall she and Sidney may have had chances to see each other, but the following January Anna was off to Europe with Granny and a chaperone, staying in splendor at the best hotels, meeting titled people, dancing with attractive young traveling Americans, meeting Mussolini, who was

then at the height of his popularity. They also had an audience with the pope. (Granny had grown up as a Unitarian,
but having an audience with the pope was "the thing to do.")
There was plenty of mail from boys back home to be read
and answered. One young hopeful, named Robert, got a letter from Anna "telling him a few things which I'm afraid he
won't appreciate much," as she said to her mother in a letter
from Rome. "I've also had loads of letters from Sidney and
several from Curt and they all seem to take it for granted
that they are the one and only in my thoughts! I don't suppose I can help that but honestly, Ma, I'm perfectly certain
that when I get home I won't be any more anxious to be
engaged than I was when I left. That doesn't mean I don't
like any of these people as much as ever but it just means
that I have so much fun with other people that I'm not in the
least ready to say I'm sure I like one person more than any
others on earth." Anna was finding it exciting to have several
beaus "on the string" and to keep them all dangling, including Sidney.

It was probably on her return from Europe that Eleanor
Roosevelt herself told Anna about her father's faithless behavior of years before; perhaps she had heard that Anna already knew. This painful conversation may have helped
Anna to make up her mind that Sidney was the man she
loved "more than any others on earth." The news of their
informal engagement was soon known in Cornwall. Sidney
was working hard on Wall Street and hoped that a formal
engagement could soon be announced. At Hyde Park,
Granny may have been kept in the dark for the time being,
but Eleanor Roosevelt knew that Sidney had become all-
important to Anna, who had an out-and-out quarrel with her
mother, protesting that she did not want to take the long-
planned course in agriculture at Cornell. The latest plan, ar-

Sidney Sherwood and Anna Roosevelt

ranged by her parents, was that Anna would spend the summer of 1925 at the State Agricultural Experimental Station in Geneva, New York. She was not consulted but was simply told that this was the best plan and must be followed.

It was too much to bear. Was she never going to decide for herself what she should do? She went to Geneva in a bad mood and spent as little time as possible on her studies. From Groton School near Boston, where Elliott, too, was wasting his time, he wrote to his parents: "Several Yale boys have been up here and have mentioned her. They think she will probably get flunked out or something like that because she never seems to be at the college at all."

It may never be known how or where Anna was spending her time that summer, but word eventually got about in the Sherwood family that Sid and Anna, like Sid's parents before them, had planned to elope, probably because it seemed that pressure from Anna's family would delay their marriage indefinitely. Then for some reason, Anna decided instead that her parents and Granny Roosevelt must be told. There is no evidence that Franklin and Eleanor Roosevelt were opposed to the match, but Granny put her foot down. A marriage between Anna and Sidney Sherwood! Impossible. It was not for nothing that Sara Delano Roosevelt had ruled the roost at Hyde Park all these years, paid bills, cared for her grandchildren during their parents' frequent absences from home, introduced Anna to the kind of life she could have if she would give up this blind folly, this irrational whim of marrying Sidney Sherwood. It is easy to picture the scene, but all that can certainly be known is the outcome. Anna promised to give up Sidney. Eleanor Roosevelt telephoned to Mary Sherwood and tried to explain, ending with "Doesn't your heart ache for those young people as mine does?" Mary repeated the conversation to an intimate friend, who passed it on to her children. Eventually a small circle in Cornwall knew about the telephone call, and it became part of the Sherwood legend.

In September, Anna entered Cornell as her parents had insisted. Then suddenly, on January 23, 1926, her engagement to Curtis Dall was announced. In June they were married and sailed to England on their honeymoon. At the same time, Sidney resigned his position with Bankers Trust Company and left for Bisbee, Arizona, to work as overseer in a copper mine owned by the Phelps Dodge Corporation, a company with strong Princeton connections. Cleveland H. Dodge, a director at the time when Sidney Sherwood went out to Bisbee, had been a classmate of Sid's father and of Woodrow Wilson. He may have played a part in giving a job to the young man who had been vice-president of the Woodrow Wilson Club at Princeton. Eleanor Roosevelt, too, may have helped with a letter of recommendation. If so, it was the first of many letters that she was to write in the years to come, recommending Sid for jobs that shaped his career, as if she not only liked him but felt that the Roosevelts owed him something. Her sincere admiration for Mary Sherwood no doubt influenced her kindness to Sid as well.

Sid's own explanation for moving to Bisbee was that he had found Wall Street "not his cup of tea." His sisters joked that he had left home to get away from them. A more likely reason for heading west was to leave behind him painful memories of Anna Roosevelt. By a quirk of fate, there were memories of Anna even at Bisbee, since she had been there only a year before.

But fate had other plans in store for Sid. The summer after he went to work for Phelps Dodge, he was called into the office of the Copper Queen mine where he worked as overseer and was asked to show some VIP visitors through the building that housed the concentrator, the apparatus used to separate copper ore from rock. As he recalled fifty years later, "there was a beautiful red-head, Olita Schlichten, the younger sister of the superintendent's wife. So I took her through, and that was the beginning of our romance. She looked out of the windows at the mountains. She wasn't interested in the milling. So we made a date to ride to the mountains. She wanted to ride all the way to the Sierra Madres, but I said that it would take four or five days. We didn't get there, but we have been going on together ever since."

As it turned out, Sid and Oly had a lifelong romance. In the Sherwood family the two were called Sid 'n' Oly, as if they were one person. Oly's family lived in Pasadena, California, and the wedding took place there in 1927. Sid's mother and Helen came from Cornwall, and Penny came from Iowa City, welcoming Oly into the bosom of the family.

The dry, clear air of Arizona should have been ideal for

Sid's health, but work underground was notoriously hard on the lungs. In any case, the stock market crash of 1929 and the onset of the Great Depression put an end to his job at Bisbee. "Last hired, first fired" was the rule. Casting about for another job, Sid again thought of fruit farming, this time in the state of Washington, where he found work in an apple orchard. It did not last. Oly later confessed that Sid had liked fruit farming better than she had. She was really a city girl, and Sid would not have wanted her to be unhappy. In 1933, once again out of a job, he took her home to Cornwall.

The most important event of that year was the inauguration of Franklin Delano Roosevelt as president of the United States. Less noticed was his daughter's failing marriage. In order to avoid bad publicity, the news was kept secret until after the inauguration. Part of the trouble between Anna and Curt was money. They had built a big house amid meadows and woods that overlooked the Hudson River. They had two children and three servants. On the surface all seemed blissful. But Curt lost heavily in the stock market crash, the property had to be sold, and Anna and Curt took refuge in the Roosevelt house in New York City. As early as 1932 when Anna traveled with her parents during the presidential campaign they knew that she was in love with John Boettiger, a newspaperman who was covering the campaign. It was arranged that when the Roosevelts moved into the White House, Anna and her two children would move in, too. As soon as the Ship of State was on an even keel, she would go to Nevada for a divorce.

The Roosevelts were in close touch with Mary Sherwood at this time because Franklin Roosevelt had asked for her help in an ugly situation at a training school for delinquent boys near Warwick, New York. It was a beautiful piece of property, but the inside story was different. Every kind of vice was present and out of control. Mary had agreed to visit the Warwick school and recommended that the boys be moved from big dormitories to cottages, where married couples could act as parents in a more homelike atmosphere, with an emphasis on job training rather than punishment. The plan worked so well that there was a complete change in the attitude and behavior of the boys. Mary Sherwood was devoted to the school and wrote regular reports to Eleanor Roosevelt, persuading her to visit Warwick herself as often as possible and see "the method of working with the boys . . . one of the cottages, the kitchen, tailor and machine shops, dairy, studio and infirmary." The two women would have lunch on the back porch at Cornwall and then drive to Warwick. Mary's letters also kept the Roosevelts in touch with the news about Sidney.

As soon as Eleanor Roosevelt heard of his return to Cornwall and his search for a job, she invited Mary to bring Sid and Oly for lunch at Hyde Park. That day the president asked Sid about his plans and learned that he would like to do something with farming. As a result, when Henry Morgenthau, Jr., a Hudson River neighbor of the Roosevelts, was appointed head of the Farm Credit Administration, he offered Sid a job. Sid and Oly immediately moved to Washington, where he became head of the Crop Production Loan Division, and quickly proved his ability as coordinator of large-scale projects. (He later said that coordinating the work of student waiters at Princeton had been good training.) By 1934 Morgenthau was Secretary of the Treasury and soon afterward made Sid coordinator for the liquor control agencies of six New England states. The disastrous prohibition era had come to an end, and Sid found himself in Boston, responsible for putting rumrunners, bootleggers, and racketeers out of business. It was an exciting job and Sid threw himself into his work with all his energy.

Three years later he fell ill with scarlet fever, followed by rheumatic fever, which sometimes leads to permanent heart damage. As he recovered, he obviously needed a vacation, and it was decided that he and Oly should have a trip abroad. Once again, Eleanor Roosevelt stepped in. She asked Joseph Kennedy, the United States ambassador to Great Britain, to arrange for Sid and Oly to meet people and see things that are usually open only to VIPs. It was Sid's first experience in international affairs. He wrote to thank Eleanor Roosevelt, who had made it possible. He was, in fact, becoming a VIP himself, due to her help, and hoped for a new appointment with greater responsibilities.

On New Year's Eve, 1939, Sid and Oly attended a dinner at the White House. On every place card was a note in Eleanor Roosevelt's hand, "You can do it!" On the back of Sidney's card she had added a special note: "Sidney, there's nothing that you cannot do, but you get it from your mother. Ha!"

With Europe at war and the United States already deeply involved, Sidney was brought back to Washington as assistant secretary of the Advisory Commission of the Council of National Defense, one of the vast networks involved in the war effort. Because of his previous experience as a coordinator, he suggested a merger of two agencies that were competing and conflicting with each other. This resulted in Sid's writing the first draft of an executive order, signed by the president, establishing the Foreign Economic Administration, which sent lend-lease supplies and strategic materials to the allies of the United States. Sid headed the Executive Policy Committee of the FEA.

Mary Sherwood began to make frequent trips to Washington, staying with Sid and Oly in their attractive apartment, where Oly was a cordial and skillful hostess to a circle of governmental and diplomatic visitors. The Sherwoods, one and all, received invitations to the White House. The first of these came shortly after Sid and Oly moved to Washington. Mary wrote to Eleanor Roosevelt that she hoped they could have tea together at Sidney's apartment. The day was set and Eleanor Roosevelt found other guests there as well, including the Morgenthaus and about a dozen other VIPs. In return came an invitation to Sid, Oly, and Mary for the ambassadors' reception. It was one of the most important formal evening events of the year, but Mary was not unprepared. She confided to a Cornwall friend that she had made a formal dress from velvet draperies stored away since Baltimore days.

With her usual good humor Mary described her entrance: "I had never been to the White House. I wore a very pretty evening dress, a long skirt with a pan velvet tunic, a lovely shade of lilac. My pumps had higher heels than I was accustomed to wearing. As we entered the porch, the rug was a little rumpled. My heel caught, and I fell, striking my nose on the floor. Bouncing up quickly, I asked Oly if my nose was bleeding. If it was, I was afraid of spotting my white gloves. Two uniformed White House aides rushed to pick me up, but were too slow. However, they insisted on getting my name to report the accident. I refused, having entirely recovered. . . . We were ushered into the Red Room, presented to the President and Mrs. Roosevelt (who wore a gorgeous red velvet gown) and Mr. and Mrs. Morgenthau, who received with the President. Then we proceeded to the spacious East Room, where a large company was assembled. Many of the foreign ambassadors were in full dress. Mrs. Roosevelt had asked Anna Roosevelt Dall to see that we met different ambassadors, which she most graciously did. . . ." This was probably the first time Sid and Anna had met since their parting fifteen years before. If it was an awkward moment, the past was evidently ignored as if it had not existed.

Gretchen, too, moved to Washington at this time, a move that may have been influenced by Sidney. She had finally realized that Columbia University would never advance her to the rank of full professor in medieval French literature and language. There was not enough interest, too few students. The State Department offered a chance to break out of this dead end. The government badly needed linguists to review for accuracy translations from French, Spanish, German, Portuguese, and Italian. Gretchen was proficient in all these languages and her long experience had made her an expert in subtle meanings as well as exact wording. The success of international negotiations depended now more than ever on deeper cultural understanding among the countries at war and would be essential for a lasting peace. As Gretchen had written twenty years earlier to Dr. Mac-Cracken of Vassar, "To arrange international matters we must *know* other nations and make allowances for differences of custom and of character." Now she was to play a small but essential part in paving the way for that understanding. She became a highly valued senior translator in the State Department and continued with them until 1960, a year before her death.

Mary Sherwood's last visit to the White House came at a luncheon party given by Eleanor Roosevelt on the back porch of the White House shortly before the president's death. It was a small party for ladies only, and included Gretchen as well as Oly, her mother, and her sister, obviously arranged out of friendship for Mary, with whom Eleanor Roosevelt never lost touch as long as she lived.

What their friendship meant to both of them can clearly be seen in the many letters that passed between them. Before each election during the Roosevelt years, Mary Sherwood sent almost motherly encouragement when Eleanor

Roosevelt badly needed it. During the campaign of 1944 Mary was asked to introduce Eleanor Roosevelt as the speaker at a Democratic rally in Newburgh. Mary was eighty years old. Mrs. Roosevelt praised her for the home she had given her children, a home that they loved to come back to from their different careers. "It was," said Mary, "the highest public honor of my life." After the election victory she wrote "Dearest Mrs. Roosevelt," rejoicing that "you and our President are to continue as our leaders for four more years," and Mrs. Roosevelt answered that "such messages give him the strength to carry on." Often she answered the same day, or within a week at the most. It is now largely forgotten how much hate mail the Roosevelts received. They were no doubt genuinely grateful for love like Mary's.

In 1945 as the Foreign Economic Administration was closing down, Sidney was well established as a leader in overseas enterprises of the United States and was called on to act as special assistant for the Export-Import Bank, a forerunner of the World Bank, which was arranging loans and encouraging independent businesses in countries all over the world. He was just beginning this demanding work when a lesion was discovered in his right lung. Tuberculosis was suspected, possibly as a result of his mining experience, but fortunately the problem was caught in time to be cured. Fortunately, too, the head of the Export-Import Bank, William McChesney Martin, thought highly enough of Sid to hold the job for him until he could return to work, at the end of 1947. During the next eleven years Sidney became an expert on Middle East economic development. He served as chief of Export-Import Bank missions in Brazil, Israel, Saudi Arabia, Lebanon, Afghanistan, Yugoslavia, and a number of western European countries. The bank was handling loans that totaled 3.5 billion dollars.

In 1959 Sidney took leave of absence to go to India as

economic attaché on the staff of the American Embassy in
New Delhi, a post where Oly shone as hostess. In his own
words, during four years there, he "advised many American
and Indian businessmen and assisted them in establishing
their joint ventures, including tire factories, aluminum, fer-
tilizer, electrical, diesel, air conditioning, engineering, and
power plants" and helped to establish the Indian Investment
Centre, designed to import capital and know-how from
abroad. At the same time he was overseeing the Export-
Import Bank's loans in Ceylon, Thailand, Pakistan, and
Afghanistan.

His father and mother could not have asked for more from
their only son. Sid himself considered his work in India to be
one of his two most important contributions. The other was
his work in coordinating defense agencies during World War
II so that the United States could speak with one voice on
foreign economic matters. He was, he said, "a firm believer
that mutual economic interest forms a solid foundation for
political understanding between nations and ultimate peaceful relations." He has not yet been proved wrong.

In 1961 Mary Sherwood told Eleanor Roosevelt that Sid
and Oly were coming home on leave from India and they
received a telegram from Hyde Park, reading, "Will you
give me an evening?" Would they give her an evening! It
would be the great event of their trip home. This time they
were not staying at 51 Angola Road. In order to save trouble
for Mary and to give her pleasure, they had made reservations at the Lake Mohonk Mountain House, a resort on a
glacial lake high in the mountains near Cornwall. Sid and
Oly drove Mary to the hotel for a day of enjoying the views
and riding by horse-drawn carriage through the spacious
grounds.

Then came the Sunday when they were to drive to Hyde

Park. At breakfast Sidney told the waitress that they would be away for dinner. He had forgotten one important fact. The resort was run by a Quaker family, the Smileys, and no one could enter or leave the grounds on Sunday. It was a day devoted to quiet meditation. Mr. Smiley was firm about it. Sidney, too, was firm, saying, "I'm sorry. This will *have* to be an exception." He produced the telegram from Eleanor Roosevelt. "Oh," Mr. Smiley said, "I know her. She comes here frequently. I've read her book [probably her autobiography] and I've decided that she's a great woman. I couldn't stand her husband. I think he ruined this country. But I do think she's a great woman." Sid answered, "Well, at least on that point you and I agree." Mr. Smiley then arranged for Sid and Oly to leave quietly through the kitchen door where they would find their car, against all the rules, waiting for them.

That night they saw Eleanor Roosevelt for the last time. She died the following year. In bidding them good-bye, she said, "You know, Sidney, every time I get discouraged, I call up your mother and ask if I can come down and have tea. She is always looking ahead." In telling this story, Sid added, "That was Mother. She gave us all courage because she had faced a hard challenge herself, raising all those babies."

Eleanor Roosevelt and Mary Sherwood had much in common. Each had a family of five children with whom she liked to go camping. Both were Democrats and were interested in public affairs. Mary had always worked for women's suffrage; Eleanor Roosevelt had had her doubts—"I took it for granted that men were superior creatures," she wrote—but once women had the vote, she became an ardent feminist and took a more and more active part in politics. Both women had high ideals, "painfully high," Eleanor Roosevelt said of herself. Both had the pain of seeing dearly loved men become alcoholics: Mary's brother; Eleanor's father, a brother, and an uncle.

Of course there were sharp contrasts, one of the obvious differences being the matter of money and position. But in some ways, not so obvious, Mary had the advantage. She was totally self-confident; Eleanor was shy all her life. Like Mary's own daughters, Eleanor had grown up without knowing boys of her own age. Mary was happy in her teenage years; Eleanor was miserable. "I rarely coasted and never skated," she wrote. Her debutante year in New York was agony. "I was a poor dancer. . . . I still remember the inappropriate dresses I wore. . . . I knew, of course, that I was different from all the other girls." Mary was a fearless rider; Eleanor was terrified of horses. Mary made an art, almost a religion, of cooking for a big tableful of people; Eleanor could hardly cook a picnic hot dog without burning it. Mary's great joy had been to play golf with the husband who adored her; Eleanor made a valiant effort to learn the game, practicing every day out of a sense of duty, only to be told by her husband that she might as well give it up. She knew that she spoiled his fun because she was never at ease, always serious, often shocked. But she was a faithful friend to rich and poor alike; the consequences of her friendships were far-reaching. In the end, she was one of the most admired women in the world. The consequences of her friendship for Mary Sherwood were examples of the difference she made in many lives.

During all the years of Sid's outstanding career, his mother's life continued almost unchanged at home. In her eighties, she was still ice skating on the pond below the house, and she still filled the house with guests. Once she said, "We've had so much company this summer, it will take me all fall to sleep through the company sheets!" She never

Mary Sherwood in happy old age in the library at 51 Angola Road

lost her sense of humor or her zest for living. One year when
Sid and Oly came home from abroad, the year when his
mother was eighty-two, Sid asked her to rent horses from a
local stable so that he and Oly could have a ride to Storm
King. She rented a third horse as well, saying, "I hope you
don't mind if I join you." She rode with them for two hours,
sitting her horse as beautifully as a girl.

And she continued to be the cook of the family. One
weekend when Jean came home for an overnight trip to
Sutherland's Pond, Sid 'n' Oly arrived at 51 Angola Road in

time for dinner, and Mary gave an unforgettable meal to celebrate the family reunion. "Magnificent!" as Jean remembered it: "Standing roast of beef, mashed potatoes and gravy, fresh peas, string beans, homemade bread, watercress from the pond with cottage cheese, olives, chili sauce, jelly, and apple pie (Ma's masterpiece!)." Grandchildren always found the cookie jar filled with fresh oatmeal cookies.

Mary died in 1963 just before her hundredth birthday. In Cornwall it seemed incredible that she was gone. No one alive in the little town could remember when she had not been part of their lives, and at least one Cornwall poet believed that she might reappear forever in and around the old house:

OVERHEARD ON ANGOLA

There she comes now, so let's wait here,
Let's sit on our sleds till she gets near.
She's old as the hills, my mother said.
Mom told me last night when I went to bed,
How in her house they had such fun,
Her children were allowed to romp and run
And have pets—all kinds—my mom said,
Even a monkey they kept in a shed!
You get your crullers at the store?
Us too; but not her; she bakes a lot more
Than you'd count, in a big black pot,
And says you can eat 'em when they're hot.
I wish my mother . . . S-sh! she's here.
You be gettin' on my sled and I'll steer.
Hi! Mis' Sherwood . . . You rode here too?
I never knew *this* hill was as old as you!

Were Mary Sherwood and her children unique in their achievements? Perhaps not. They were part of the American middle-class culture in which effort and personal fulfillment matter, and commitment to service matters even more. There was in them what Americans like to think of as the essential American character, the will to make a difference, each in his or her own way. But in one thing they were almost unique. Though many widowed mothers have brought up their families on less money than Mary had, when simplicity of life was forced upon the Sherwoods by circumstances, they made it a beautiful thing. In this they were enviable. Eleanor Roosevelt once wrote to Anna, "What a lot of fun people who never had much get out of things, don't they?" She may have been thinking of the Sherwoods.

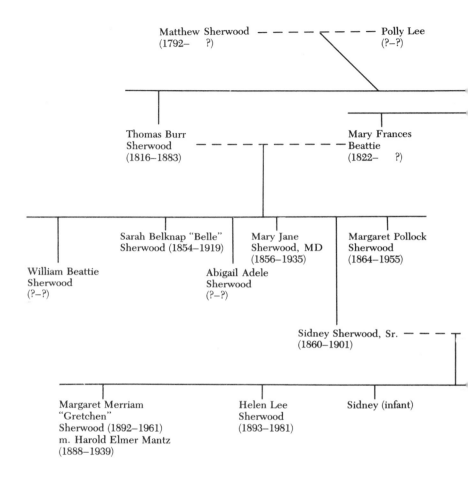

Matthew Sherwood — — — — ⌐ — — — Polly Lee
(1792–   ?)   (?–?)

Thomas Burr
Sherwood   — — — — — — ⊤ — — — — — Mary Frances
(1816–1883)   Beattie
                                                          (1822–   ?)

Sarah Belknap "Belle"   Mary Jane   Margaret Pollock
Sherwood (1854–1919)   Sherwood, MD   Sherwood
                                              (1856–1935)   (1864–1955)

William Beattie   Abigail Adele
Sherwood   Sherwood
(?–?)   (?–?)

                                                          Sidney Sherwood, Sr. — — — ⊤
                                                          (1860–1901)

Margaret Merriam   Helen Lee   Sidney (infant)
"Gretchen"   Sherwood
Sherwood (1892–1961)   (1893–1981)
m. Harold Elmer Mantz
(1888–1939)

SOME ROOTS AND BRANCHES
OF A FAMILY TREE

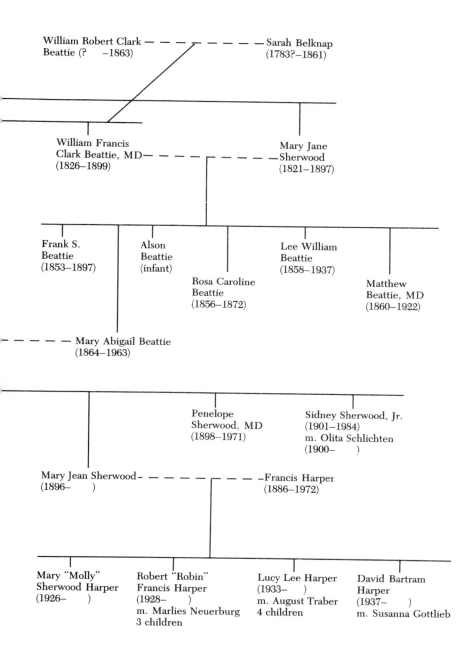

William Robert Clark Beattie (? –1863) — — — — — — — Sarah Belknap (1783?–1861)

William Francis Clark Beattie, MD (1826–1899) — — — — — — — Mary Jane Sherwood (1821–1897)

Frank S. Beattie (1853–1897)

Alson Beattie (infant)

Rosa Caroline Beattie (1856–1872)

Lee William Beattie (1858–1937)

Matthew Beattie, MD (1860–1922)

— — — — — Mary Abigail Beattie (1864–1963)

Penelope Sherwood. MD (1898–1971)

Sidney Sherwood, Jr. (1901–1984) m. Olita Schlichten (1900–)

Mary Jean Sherwood (1896–) — — — — — — — Francis Harper (1886–1972)

Mary "Molly" Sherwood Harper (1926–)

Robert "Robin" Francis Harper (1928–) m. Marlies Neuerburg 3 children

Lucy Lee Harper (1933–) m. August Traber 4 children

David Bartram Harper (1937–) m. Susanna Gottlieb

INDEX